Plain English
for Lawyers

Plain English for Lawyers

FIFTH EDITION

Richard C. Wydick

EMERITUS PROFESSOR OF LAW
UNIVERSITY OF CALIFORNIA, DAVIS

CAROLINA ACADEMIC PRESS
Durham, North Carolina

Library of Congress Cataloging-in-Publication Data

Wydick, Richard C.
Plain English for lawyers / by Richard C. Wydick. -- 5th ed.
p. cm.
Includes bibliographical references and index.
ISBN 1-59460-151-8 (alk. paper)
1. Legal composition. I. Title.

KF250.W9 2005
808'.06634--dc22

2005016369

CAROLINA ACADEMIC PRESS
700 Kent Street
Durham, North Carolina 27701
Telephone (919) 489-7486
Fax (919) 493-5668
www.cap-press.com

Printed in the United States of America

To JJW, with love

Contents

Preface and Acknowledgments

The first edition of *Plain English for Lawyers* was a revised version of an article that appeared in 66 California Law Review 727, published by the students of the University of California, Berkeley, School of Law, copyright 1978, by the California Law Review, Inc.

Many of the changes made in subsequent editions reflect the ideas, writings, and suggestions made by others who toil in the field of legal writing. My debts to them are so many that to acknowledge all of them properly in footnotes or endnotes would distract the reader— a sin that all of us in the field preach against. Thus, let me here thank my scholarly creditors including the following: Kenneth Adams, Mark Adler, Robert Benson, Norman Brand, Robert Chaim, Robert Charrow, Veda Charrow, Martin Cutts, Robert Eagleson, J.M. Foers, Bryan Garner, Tom Goldstein, George Hathaway, Margaret Johns, Joseph Kimble, Philip Knight, Jethro Lieberman, Ray Parnas, Janice Redish, Peter Tiersma, Richard Thomas, and Garth Thornton. Thanks also to Keltie Jones for her fine work on the punctuation chapter.

I owe special thanks to David Mellinkoff, who died on the last day of the 20th century. He was educated at Stanford University and Harvard Law School. After serving as an artillery officer in World War II, he became a successful practicing lawyer in Beverly Hills and later a beloved law professor at UCLA. All of us in the field of legal writing have benefitted from his careful scholarship and wise guidance expressed in *The Language of the Law* (1963), *Legal Writing:*

Sense & Nonsense (1982), and *Mellinkoff's Dictionary of American Legal Usage* (1992).

Richard C. Wydick
Davis, California
June 2005

Plain English
for Lawyers

Chapter 1

Why Plain English?

We lawyers do not write plain English. We use eight words to say what could be said in two. We use arcane phrases to express commonplace ideas. Seeking to be precise, we become redundant. Seeking to be cautious, we become verbose. Our sentences twist on, phrase within clause within clause, glazing the eyes and numbing the minds of our readers. The result is a writing style that has, according to one critic, four outstanding characteristics. It is "(1) wordy, (2) unclear, (3) pompous, and (4) dull."[1]

Criticism of legal writing is nothing new. In 1596, an English chancellor decided to make an example of a particularly prolix document filed in his court. The chancellor first ordered a hole cut through the center of the document, all 120 pages of it. Then he ordered that the person who wrote it should have his head stuffed through the hole, and the unfortunate fellow was led around to be exhibited to all those attending court at Westminster Hall.[2]

When the common law was transplanted to America, the writing style of the old English lawyers came with it. In 1817 Thomas Jefferson lamented that in drafting statutes his fellow lawyers were accustomed to "making every other word a 'said' or 'aforesaid' and saying everything over two or three times, so that nobody but we of the craft can untwist the diction and find out what it means...."[3]

Legal writing style long remained a subject of jokes and ridicule, but a reform movement started in the 1970s. A few legislatures passed laws that require documents such as insurance policies and consumer contracts to be written in plain language. Banks, manufacturers, and other businesses discovered that documents written in plain language can reduce costs and increase profits. For example, an auto maker's clearly written warranty can help sell cars, and a lender's clearly written loan agreement can reduce costly defaults and foreclosures. Understandable government forms can reduce the amount of staff time spent answering questions from puzzled citizens.

The movement toward plain legal language is changing the legal profession itself. Most law schools now teach the plain language style in their legal writing courses. Court rules, such as the Federal Rules of Appellate Procedure, have been rewritten to make them easier for lawyers and judges to use. Diligent committees of experts are rewriting packaged jury instructions to help make legal doctrines understandable to the jurors who must apply them. Practicing lawyers become eager students in continuing legal education courses that teach clear writing.

Our profession has made progress, yes, but the victory is not yet won. Too many law students report back from their first jobs that the plain language style they learned in law school is not acceptable to the older lawyers for whom they work. Too many estate planning clients leave their lawyer's office with a will and trust agreement in hand, but without fully understanding what they say. Too many people merely skim, or even ignore, the dense paragraphs of securities disclosures, credit card agreements, apartment leases, cell phone contracts, and promissory notes, preferring to rely on the integrity or mercy of the author rather than to struggle with the author's legal prose.

The premise of this book is that good legal writing should not differ, without good reason, from ordinary well-written English.[4] As a well-known New York lawyer told the young associates in his firm, "Good legal writing does not sound as though it had been written by a lawyer."

In short, good legal writing is plain English. Here is an example of plain English, the statement of facts from the majority opinion in *Palsgraf v. Long Island Railroad Co.*,[5] written by Benjamin Cardozo:

> Plaintiff was standing on a platform of defendant's railroad after buying a ticket to go to Rockaway Beach. A train stopped at the station, bound for another place. Two men ran forward to catch it. One of the men reached the platform of the car without mishap, though the train was already moving. The other man, carrying a package, jumped aboard the car, but seemed unsteady as if about to fall. A guard on the car, who had held the door open, reached forward to help him in, and another guard on the platform pushed him from behind. In this act, the package was dislodged and fell upon the rails. It was a package of small size, about fifteen inches long, and was covered by newspaper. In fact it contained fireworks, but there was nothing in its appearance to give notice of its contents. The fireworks when they fell exploded. The shock of the explosion threw down some scales at the other end of the platform many feet away. The scales struck the plaintiff, causing injuries for which she sues.

What distinguishes the writing style in this passage from that found in most legal writing? Notice Justice Cardozo's economy of words. He does not say "despite the fact that the train was already moving." He says "though the train was already moving."

Notice his choice of words. He uses no archaic phrases, no misty abstractions, no hereinbefore's.

Notice his care in arranging words. There are no wide gaps between the subjects and their verbs, nor between the verbs and their objects. There are no ambiguities to leave us wondering who did what to whom.

Notice his use of verbs. Most of them are in the simple form, and all but two are in the active voice.

Notice the length and construction of his sentences. Most of them contain only one main thought, and they vary in length: the shortest is six words, and the longest is twenty-seven words. These and other elements of plain English style are discussed in this book. But you cannot learn to write plain English by reading a book. You must put your own pencil to paper. That is why practice exercises are included at the end of each section. When you finish the section, work the exercises. Then compare your results with those suggested in the Appendix at the end of the book.

Notes

1. David Mellinkoff, *The Language of the Law* 23 (Little, Brown 1963).

2. *Mylward v. Welden* (Ch. 1596), reprinted in C. Monro, *Acta Cancellariae* 692 (1847). Joseph Kimble has pointed out that the person who wrote, and subsequently wore, the offending document may have been the plaintiff's son, a non-lawyer. Professor Kimble dryly notes that the son was probably following a lawyer's form. Joseph Kimble, *Plain English: A Charter for Clear Writing*, 9 Cooley L. Rev. 1, n. 2 (1992), relying on Michele M. Asprey, *Plain Language for Lawyers* 31 (Federation Press 1991).

3. Letter to Joseph C. Cabell (Sept. 9, 1817), reprinted in 17 *Writings of Thomas Jefferson* 417–18 (A. Bergh ed. 1907).

4. This premise is taken from David Mellinkoff, *The Language of the Law* vii; see also David Mellinkoff, *Dictionary of American Legal Usage* vii (West 1992).

5. 248 N.Y. 339, 162 N.E. 99 (1928). I have used *Palsgraf* as an example because it is familiar to all who have studied law. In general, however, Justice Cardozo's writing style is too ornate for modern tastes. For good examples of modern plain English style, examine the opinions of former United States Supreme Court Justice Lewis F. Powell or United States Circuit Judge Richard Posner.

Chapter 2

Omit Surplus Words

As a beginning lawyer, I was assigned to assist an older man, a business litigator. He hated verbosity. When I would bring him what I thought was a finished piece of work, he would read it quietly and take out his pen. As I watched over his shoulder, he would strike out whole lines, turn clauses into phrases, and turn phrases into single words. One day at lunch, I asked him how he did it. He shrugged and said, "It's not hard—just omit the surplus words."

How to Spot Bad Construction

In every English sentence are two kinds of words: working words and glue words. The working words carry the meaning of the sentence. In the preceding sentence the working words are these: *working, words, carry, meaning,* and *sentence.* The others are glue words: *the, the, of,* and *the.* The glue words do perform a vital service. They hold the working words together to form a proper, grammatical sentence.[1] Without them, the sentence would read like a telegram. But if the *proportion* of glue words is too high, that is a symptom of a badly constructed sentence.

A well constructed sentence is like fine cabinetwork. The pieces are cut and shaped to fit together with scarcely any glue. When you find too many glue words in a sentence, take it apart and reshape the pieces to fit together tighter. Consider this example:

7

A trial by jury was requested by the defendant.

If the working words are underlined, the sentence looks like this:

A <u>trial</u> by <u>jury</u> was <u>requested</u> by the <u>defendant</u>.

Five words in that nine-word sentence are glue: *a, by, was, by,* and *the.* That proportion of glue words is too high.

How can we say the same thing in a tighter sentence with less glue? First, move *defendant* to the front and make it the subject of the sentence. Second, use *jury trial* in place of *trial by jury.* The sentence would thus read:

The defendant requested a jury trial.

If the working words are underlined, the rewritten sentence looks like this:

The <u>defendant</u> <u>requested</u> a <u>jury</u> <u>trial</u>.

Again there are four working words, but the glue words have been cut from five to two. The sentence means the same as the original, but it is tighter and one-third shorter.

Here is another example:

The ruling by the trial judge was prejudicial error for the reason that it cut off cross-examination with respect to issues that were vital.

If the working words are underlined, we have:

The <u>ruling</u> by the <u>trial</u> <u>judge</u> was <u>prejudicial</u> <u>error</u> for the <u>reason</u> that it <u>cut</u> <u>off</u> <u>cross-examination</u> with respect to <u>issues</u> that were <u>vital</u>.

In a sentence of twenty-four words, eleven carry the meaning and thirteen are glue. Again, the proportion of glue is too high.

Note the string of words *the ruling by the trial judge.* That tells us that it was the trial judge's ruling. Why not just say *the trial judge's ruling?* The same treatment will tighten the words at the end of the sentence. *Issues that were vital* tells us that they were vital issues. Why not say *vital issues?* Now note the phrase *for the reason that.* Does it say any more than *because?* If not, we can use one word in place of four. Likewise, *with respect to* can be reduced to *on.* Rewritten, the sentence looks like this:

> The trial judge's ruling was prejudicial error because it cut off cross-examination on vital issues.

Here it is with the working words underlined:

> The <u>trial</u> <u>judge's</u> <u>ruling</u> was <u>prejudicial</u> <u>error</u> because it <u>cut</u> <u>off</u> <u>cross-examination</u> on <u>vital</u> <u>issues</u>.

The revised sentence uses fifteen words in place of the original twenty-four, and ten of the fifteen are working words. The revised sentence is both tighter and stronger than the original.

Consider a third example, but this time use a pencil and paper to rewrite the sentence yourself.

> In many instances, insofar as the jurors are concerned, the jury instructions are not understandable because they are too poorly written.

Does your sentence trim the phrase *in many instances?* Here the single word *often* will suffice. Does your sentence omit the phrase *insofar as the jurors are concerned?* That adds bulk but little meaning. Finally, did you find a way to omit the clumsy *because* clause at the end of the sentence? Your rewritten sentence should look something like this:

> Often jury instructions are too poorly written for the jurors to understand.

Here it is with the working words underlined:

> <u>Often</u> <u>jury</u> <u>instructions</u> are <u>too</u> <u>poorly</u> <u>written</u> for the <u>jurors</u> to <u>understand.</u>

The rewritten sentence is nine words shorter than the original, and eight of its twelve words are working words.

❧ Exercise 1

Underline the working words in the sentences below. Note the proportion of glue words to working words. Next, rewrite the sentences, underline the working words, and compare your results with the original sentences. Then look at the exercise key in the Appendix at the back of the book.

1. There are three reasons given in the majority opinion for its rejection of the approach taken by the Supreme Court in its earlier decisions with respect to the Confrontation Clause of the Sixth Amendment.

2. A motion has been made by Erickson seeking severance of his case from the action against Orrick and the proceedings against Sims, and for a trial of his case separate from the trial of the other two cases.

3. When entering into an agreement regarding the settlement of a claim made by a client, a lawyer must not offer or agree to a provision that imposes a restriction of the right of the lawyer to practice law, including the right to undertake representation of or take particular actions on behalf of other clients or potential clients with similar claims.

4. The conclusion that was reached in 1954 by the United States Supreme Court in the case of *Brown v. Board of Education of Topeka* was that the maintenance of a "separate but equal" education system in which segregation of children in the public schools solely on the basis of race is practiced, notwithstanding the fact that the physical facilities and other tangible factors of the separate schools might be, or were in fact, equal, brings about a deprivation of the children from

the minority group of equal opportunities with respect to education and thus causes a denial of equal protection of the laws, which is guaranteed to those children by the Fourteenth Amendment.

Avoid Compound Constructions

Compound constructions use three or four words to do the work of one or two words. They suck the vital juices from your writing. You saw some examples in the last section. *With respect to* was used instead of *on*. *For the reason that* was used instead of *because*.

Every time you see one of these pests on your page, swat it. Use a simple form instead. Here is a list of examples:

Compound	Simple
at that point in time	then
by means of	by
by reason of	because of
by virtue of	by, under
for the purpose of	to
for the reason that	because
in accordance with	by, under
inasmuch as	since
in connection with	with, about, concerning
in favor of	for
in order to	to
in relation to	about, concerning
in the event that	if
in the nature of	like
prior to	before
subsequent to	after
with a view to	to
with reference to	about, concerning

℃ᴗ Exercise 2

Use one or two words to replace the compound constructions in these sentences. Then look at the exercise key in the Appendix at the back of the book.

● 1. For the purpose of controlling how his art collection could be displayed subsequent to his death, the doctor created a very restrictive trust with a view to keeping everything exactly as it was during his lifetime.

2. In relation to the enormous charitable gift deduction claimed by the taxpayer, inasmuch as she failed to submit an appraiser's report with reference to the donated bronze sculpture, we propose to disallow the deduction in accordance with the Revenue Department's standard operating procedure.

● 3. The relief sought by plaintiff in connection with this case is in the nature of a mandatory injunction; prior to the merger of law and equity, such relief could be granted only by Chancery.

● 4. At this point in time, no legal remedy is available due to the fact that the statute of limitations has run.

5. On the basis of the affidavits filed by plaintiff and defendants with reference to the cross-motions for summary judgment, we have reached the conclusion that there are contested issues of fact, and in accordance with that conclusion, no summary judgment can be issued at this particular time.

6. From the point of view of judicial economy, our submission to the court is that it should consolidate all nine of the civil actions, both for the purpose of discovery at the present time, and at a later time for the purpose of trial.

Avoid Word-Wasting Idioms

Once you develop a distaste for surplus words, you will find many word-wasting idioms to trim from your sentences with no loss of meaning. For instance:

The fact that the defendant was young may have influenced the jury.

What meaning does *the fact that* add? Why not say:

The defendant's youth may have influenced the jury.

The fact that is almost always surplus. See how it can be trimmed from these examples:

Verbose	Concise
the fact that she had died	her death
he was aware of the fact that	he knew that
despite the fact that	although, even though
because of the fact that	because

Likewise, words like *case, instance,* and *situation* spawn verbosity:

Verbose	Concise
in some instances the parties can	sometimes the parties can
in many cases you will find	often you will find
that was a situation in which the court	there the court
disability claims are now more frequent than was formerly the case	disability claims are more frequent now

injunctive relief is required in the situation in which	injunctive relief is required when
in the majority of instances the grantor will	usually the grantor will

Other examples of common word-wasting idioms that you can eliminate with no loss of meaning are:

Verbose	Concise
during the time that	during, while
for the period of	for
insofar as … is concerned	(omit it and start with the subject)
there is no doubt but that	doubtless, no doubt
the question as to whether	whether, the question whether
this is a topic that	this topic
until such time as	until

℘ Exercise 3

Revise these examples to omit the word-wasting idioms and other surplus words. Then look at the exercise key in the Appendix at the back of the book.

- 1. Pursuant to the terms of the copyright license …

- 2. At such time as the escrow closes …

- 3. This is a situation in which mandatory injunctive relief is inappropriate …

- 4. Subsequent to her release from prison, she was confined at home for a period not less than six months.

- 5. There can be no doubt but that His Honor is required to recuse himself.

6. The action was barred by reason of the expiration of the time period specified by the statute of limitations.

7. The Court of Appeal must give consideration to the question as to whether …

8. Until such time as the plans receive the approval of the design review committee, commencement of construction is prohibited by the rules adopted by the homeowner association.

9. In the majority of instances, the insurance adjuster will, at the outset, deny the claim.

● 10. Instigation of a law suit in the absence of a good faith belief that the underlying claim is supported by a sound legal and factual basis can result in professional discipline of the attorney, in addition to the imposition of litigation sanctions on both the attorney and on the client as well.

Focus on the Actor, the Action, and the Object

One way to remedy a wordy, fogbound sentence is to ask yourself: "Who is doing what to whom in this sentence?"[2] Then rewrite the sentence to focus on those three key elements—the actor, the action, and the object of the action (if there is an object). First, state the actor. Then, state the action, using the strongest verb that will fit. Last, state the object of the action, if there is an object. Here is a simple example:

It is possible for the court to modify the judgment.

The actor is *court*, the action is *modify*, and the object of the action is *judgment*. What is the purpose of the first four words in the sentence? None. Not only are they wasted words, but they preempt the most important position in the sentence—the beginning— where the reader wants to find the actor and the action.

The sentence is both shorter and stronger when it is rewritten to focus on the actor, the action, and the object:

The court can modify the judgment.

Be alert when you find a sentence or clause that begins with *it* or *there*, followed by a form of the verb *to be*. Does the *it* or *there* refer to something specific? If not, you may be wasting words. Consider this passage:

The summons arrived this morning. It is on your desk.

The second sentence begins with *it*, followed by *is*, a form of the verb to be. The sentence is not faulty, however, because the *it* obviously refers back to *summons* in the prior sentence. But what does the *it* refer to in the following sentence?

It is obvious that the summons was not properly served.

The *it* does not refer to anything specific; rather, it points off into the fog somewhere. The sentence should be revised to read:

Obviously the summons was not properly served.

Here is a final example:

There were no reasons offered by the court for denying punitive damages.

Note that *there* is followed by *were*, a form of the verb *to be*. The *there* points off into the fog. The actor in the sentence is *court*, but it is hidden away in the middle of the sentence. The sentence would be shorter and stronger if it read:

The court offered no reasons for denying punitive damages.

∾ Exercise 4

Focus on the actor, the action, and the object (if there is one) when you rewrite these sentences. Also, omit as many surplus words as you can. Then look at the exercise key in the Appendix.

1. There are three interrelated reasons that might be the motivation for a person to make a gift of significant size to a charitable organization.

2. One reason might be simply that the person is motivated by a desire to benefit the charity in question.

3. Avoidance of the capital gains tax is a second reason why a person might make a gift to charity of an asset that has sharply increased in value since the date of its acquisition by the person.

4. In the event that the person is exceedingly wealthy, a third reason for a large charitable donation might be the desire to lessen the amount of estate taxes that would be imposed upon the person's estate at the time of his or her death.

5. It is important for tax lawyers and estate planners to show their clients the multiple ways in which a person's natural desire to achieve the gratification of having made a gift to charity can produce beneficial results at tax time as well.

Do Not Use Redundant Legal Phrases

Why do lawyers use the term *null and void*? According to the dictionary, either *null* or *void* by itself would do the job. But the lawyer's pen seems impelled to write *null and void*, as though driven by primordial instinct. An occasional lawyer, perhaps believing that *null and void* looks naked by itself, will write *totally null and void*, or perhaps *totally null and void and of no further force or effect whatsoever*.

The phrase *null and void* is an example of coupled synonyms—
a pair or string of words with the same or nearly the same meaning.[3] Here are other common examples:

alter or change	last will and testament
confessed and acknowl- edged	made and entered into
convey, transfer, and set over	order and direct
for and during the period	peace and quiet
force and effect	rest, residue, and remainder
free and clear	save and except
full and complete	suffer or permit
give, devise and bequeath	true and correct
good and sufficient	undertake and agree

Coupled synonyms have ancient roots. Some of them come
from the days when lawyers in England needed to make themselves
understood to both the courts (which used Latin and later law
French) and to common folk (who used Old English and later
Middle English).[4] For example, *free and clear* comes from the Old
English *freo* and the Old French *cler*. Other coupled synonyms are
alliterative, which means that the joined terms begin with the same
sound, like *to have and to hold*. In the days when many legal trans-
actions were oral, the alliteration was an aid to memory.[5] Still
other coupled synonyms served a rhetorical purpose.[6] That is, they
used to sound impressive, like *ordered, adjudged, and decreed*.[7]
Whatever their origin, coupled synonyms became traditional in
legal language, and they persist today, long after any practical purpose has died.

Ask a modern lawyer why he or she uses a term like *suffer or permit* in a simple apartment lease. The first answer will likely be: "for
precision." True, *suffer* has a slightly different meaning than its companion *permit*. But *suffer* in this sense is now rare in ordinary usage,
and *permit* would do the job if it were used alone.

The lawyer might then tell you that *suffer or permit* is better because it is a traditional legal term of art. Traditional it may be, but a term of art it is not. A term of art is a short expression that (a) conveys a fairly well-agreed meaning, and (b) saves the many words that would otherwise be needed to convey that meaning. *Suffer or permit* fails to satisfy the second condition, and perhaps the first as well.

The word *hearsay* is an example of a true term of art. First, its core meaning is well agreed in modern evidence law, although its meaning at the margin has always inspired scholarly debate.[8] Second, *hearsay* enables a lawyer to use one word instead of many to say that a person's statement is being offered into evidence to prove that what it asserts is true, and that the statement is not one the person made while testifying at the trial or hearing. One word that can say all that deserves our praise and deference. But *suffer or permit* does not.

Suffer or permit probably found its way into that apartment lease because the lawyer was working from a form that had been used around the office for years. The author of the form, perhaps long dead, probably worked from some even older form that might, in turn, have been inspired by a formbook or some now defunct appellate case where the phrase was used but not examined.

If you want your writing to have a musty, formbook smell, by all means use as many coupled synonyms as you can find. If you want it to be crisp, use few or none.[9] When one looms up on your page, stop to see if one of the several words, or perhaps a fresh word, will carry your intended meaning. You will find, for example, that the phrase *last will and testament* can be replaced by the single word *will*.[10]

This is not as simple as it sounds. Lawyers are busy, cautious people, and they cannot afford to make mistakes. The old, redundant phrase has worked in the past; a new one may somehow raise a question. To check it in the law library will take time, and time is the lawyer's most precious commodity. But remember—once you slay one of these old monsters, it will stay dead for the rest of your legal career. If your memory is short, keep a card or computer file of slain redundancies. Such trophies distinguish a lawyer from a scrivener.

ᏉᏉ Exercise 5

● In the following passage you will find all the kinds of surplus words discussed in chapter 2. Rewrite the passage, omitting as many surplus words as you can. Then look at the exercise key in the Appendix at the back of the book.

> It cannot be gainsaid that one of the primary obligations owed by an agent to his or her principal is to act with the degree of carefulness, competence, and diligent devotion to duty that are normally exercised by and/or employed by agents of ordinary skill and prudence in like or similar circumstances. In the situation in which the agent in question is possessed of special skills and/or knowledge, that is a factor to be taken into account in reaching a determination whether the agent in question did or did not act in accordance with the legal standard of due care and diligence. Moreover, it goes without saying that it is the duty of an agent to undertake a course of action only within the metes and bounds of the actual authority granted by the principal to the agent. It is the duty of an agent to act in compliance with all instructions that are within the bounds of the law and that are received from either the principal himself or persons theretofore designated by the principal as respects actions taken by the agent for or on behalf of the principal.

Notes

1. My distinction between working words and glue words is neither profound nor precise, and reasonable people can disagree about whether a given word in

a sentence is a working word or a glue word. If the distinction is helpful to you, use it as a tool, but don't think it's scientific or sacred. About fifteen years after cooking up my distinction, I found a similar distinction between "content words" and "function words" in the writings of Harvard cognition and language expert Steven Pinker. Function words, Professor Pinker writes, "are bits of crystallized grammar ... [that provide] a scaffolding for the sentence." Steven Pinker, *The Language Instinct* 118 (William Morrow & Co. 1994). Content words, on the other hand, are words like *sailboat, remember, purple,* and similar nouns, verbs, adjectives, and adverbs that express the substance of the sentence. *See id.* at 47, 117–20. Pinker invites his readers to consider whether the two types of words are supplied by different parts of the human brain. *See id.* at 45–53; *see also,* Steven Pinker, *Words and Rules* 1, 92–133 (Phoenix 1999). Another similar distinction is made by grammar expert Randolph Quirk and his co-authors. *See* Robert A. Chaim, *A Model for the Analysis of the Language of Lawyers* 33 J. Legal Educ. 120 (1983). They divide parts of speech into "closed classes" and "open classes." The closed classes (roughly similar to my glue words) include prepositions, pronouns, articles, demonstratives, conjunctions, modal verbs (like *can, must,* and *will*) and primary verbs (like *be, have,* and *do*). The closed classes contain relatively few words, and normally new words can't qualify for membership. In contrast, the open classes (roughly similar to my working words) include nouns, adjectives, adverbs, and full verbs (like *steal, build,* and *haggle*). The open classes welcome newcomers, which keeps bread on the tables of dictionary makers. *See* Randolph Quirk, Sidney Greenbaum, Geoffrey Leech, and Jan Svartvik, *A Comprehensive Grammar of the English Language* 67–75 (Addison Wesley 1985).

2. This prescription is part of a "Paramedic Method" devised by Professor Richard A. Lanham for rendering first aid to sick sentences. *See* Richard A. Lanham, *Revising Prose* 15–21(4th ed., Allyn & Bacon 2000). *See also* Joseph M. Williams, *Style: Toward Clarity and Grace* 27–40 (Univ. of Chicago 1995).

3. *See* Bryan A. Garner, *A Dictionary of Modern Legal Usage* 292–295 (2nd ed., Oxford 1995); David Mellinkoff, *Mellinkoff's Dictionary of American Legal Usage* 129–132 (West 1992).

4. *See* Peter M. Tiersma, *Legal Language* 10–17 (Chicago 1999); David Mellinkoff, *The Language of the Law* 38–39, 121–22 (Little, Brown 1963).

5. Tiersma, *Legal Language* at 13–15.

6. Garner, *A Dictionary of Modern Legal Usage* at 292.

7. *Id.* at 292, 625. The three terms *ordered, adjudged, and decreed* once had slightly different meanings, but Garner says that the single term *ordered* will usually suffice. *Id.* at 625.

8. *See* Fed. R. Evid. 801(c); *McCormick on Evidence* §§ 246–51 (John W. Strong gen. ed., 5th ed. West 1999).

9. David Mellinkoff notes that a few coupled synonyms have become so "welded by usage" that they act as a single term. These few are tolerable, he says, when used in the proper context. Mellinkoff, *Mellinkoff's Dictionary of American Legal Usage*

at 129–32. For example, *pain and suffering* is acceptable in tort pleadings, and *full faith and credit* is acceptable in a brief or opinion on that constitutional clause.

10. Bryan Garner says that *last will and testament* is a ceremonial phrase that does no harm when used as the title of a client's will. But, Garner says, if you were writing a brief or an opinion about someone's will, you should call it just plain *will*, not *last will and testament*. *See* Garner, *A Dictionary of Modern Legal Usage* at 294–95, 500.

Chapter 3

Use Base Verbs,
Not Nominalizations

At its core, the law is not abstract. It is part of a real world full of people who live and move and do things to other people. Car drivers *collide*. Plaintiffs *complain*. Judges *decide*. Defendants *pay*.

To express this life and motion, a writer must use verbs—action words. The purest verb form is the base verb, like *collide, complain, decide,* and *pay*. Base verbs are simple creatures. They cannot tolerate adornment. If you try to dress them up, you squash their life and motion. The base verb *collide* can be decked out as a noun, *collision*. Likewise, *complain* becomes *complaint*. *Decide* becomes *decision*. *Pay* becomes *payment*.

A base verb that has been turned into a noun is called a "nominalization." Lawyers and bureaucrats love nominalizations. Lawyers and bureaucrats do not *act*—they *take action*. They do not *assume*—they *make assumptions*. They do not *conclude*—they *draw conclusions*.

If you use nominalizations instead of base verbs, surplus words begin to swarm like gnats. "Please *state* why you *object* to the question," comes out like this: "Please *make a statement* of why you are *interposing an objection* to the question." The base verb *state* can do the work all alone. But to get the same work out of *statement*, you need a supporting verb (*make*), an article (*a*), and a preposition (*of*). The word *objection* attracts a similar cloud of surplus words.

23

You can spot most of the common nominalizations by their endings:

-al	-ment	-ant
-ence	-ion	-ent
-ancy	-ency	-ance
-ity		

Not all words with those endings are nominalizations. Further, not all nominalizations are bad. Sometimes you cannot avoid them. But do not overuse them; when you find one on your page, stop to see if you can make your sentence shorter and stronger by using a base verb instead.

❧ Exercise 6

Revise these sentences, omitting surplus words and, where possible, using base verbs in place of nominalizations. Then look at the exercise key in the Appendix.

1. Rejection of an insurance policy holder's facially valid claim is not an action that an insurance claims agent should undertake lightly.

2. Rather, the claims agent should give careful consideration to the possible consequences.

3. A term by implication in *every* contract is that the parties have a duty of good faith and fair dealing, and insurance contracts are no exception.

4. A claims agent's blunt refusal to provide any reasoned explanation for his failure to make any payment on a facially valid claim raises a question in our minds about the agent's good faith.

● 5. Fulfillment of the duty of good faith by the insurance company has as one of its requirements an obligation to provide a coherent response to a facially valid claim.

● 6. The continuation of the claims agent's "stonewall" tactic for a period of 10 months leads us to the inference that the agent's intention was to stall until the policy holder's capitulation or engagement of a lawyer.

Chapter 4

Prefer the Active Voice

The Difference Between Active and Passive Voice

When you use a verb in the active voice, the subject of the sentence does the acting. "John kicks the ball," is in the active voice. *John* is the subject, and John does the acting: he kicks the ball. When you use a verb in the passive voice, the subject of the sentence is acted upon. "The ball is kicked by John," is in the passive voice. *Ball* is the subject, and the ball is being acted upon: it is kicked by John.

Active
John kicked the ball.

Passive
The ball was kicked by John.

The two sentences mean the same thing, but observe that the sentence in the passive voice is longer than the sentence in the active voice. In the active voice, the single word *kicks* expresses the action all by itself. The passive voice needs three words, *is kicked by*, to express the same action. Thus, one good reason to prefer the active voice is economy—the active voice takes fewer words. Notice that in each of the following examples, the active voice takes fewer words than the passive voice:

Active Voice
The union filed a complaint
The trial judge will deny your motion.
The legislative history supports our conclusion.
The trustor had not intended the trust to ...

Passive Voice
A complaint was filed by the union.
Your motion will be denied by the trial judge.
Our conclusion is supported by the legislative history.
The trust had not been intended by the trustor to ...

Both the active voice and the passive voice can express action in various tenses, that is, action at various times. For example:

Active	Passive
John kicked the ball.	The ball was kicked by John.
John kicks the ball.	The ball is kicked by John.
John will kick the ball.	The ball will be kicked by John.
John has kicked the ball.	The ball has been kicked by John.
John had kicked the ball.	The ball had been kicked by John.
John will have kicked the ball.	The ball will have been kicked by John.

No matter what the verb tense—past, present, future, or something more complicated—the key difference between the active and passive voice remains the same: in the active voice, the subject of the sentence does the acting, but in the passive voice, the subject of the sentence is acted upon.

⚬ Exercise 7

First, underline the verbs in these sentences. (Note that all the sentences have more than one verb.) Next, identify each verb as either active voice or passive voice. Then look at the exercise key in the Appendix.

1. The new state statute <u>required</u> Blanchard to <u>register</u> as a sex offender because, thirty-five years earlier, he <u>had been con-victed</u> of <u>forcing</u> a minor to orally <u>copulate</u> him, a felony.

2. Twelve years after Blanchard <u>was released</u> from prison for that first offense, he <u>brandished</u> a stick at an armored police vehicle during an anti-abortion demonstration, for which he <u>was convicted</u> of a felony—threatening serious bodily harm to a police officer. He <u>served</u> 18 months in state prison for that offense, and he <u>was released</u> in 1987.

3. On June 30th of last year, the new sex offender registration statute <u>went</u> into effect. It <u>required</u> Blanchard to register within 30 days, and Blanchard <u>did so</u> on July 15th.

4. The registration statute <u>requires</u> every registered person to "update" the registration within five days following his or her birthday. Blanchard's birthday <u>is</u> July 17th. Nothing significant <u>happened</u> in Blanchard's life between July 15th and July 30th. Neither his address, nor his telephone number, nor his employment, nor any of his other registration data <u>changed</u> between those two dates.

5. On July 30th, Blanchard <u>was arrested</u> by Police Lieutenant Lacy (one of the officers who <u>was sitting</u> in the armored police vehicle when Blanchard <u>brandished</u> the stick many years earlier). Blanchard <u>was arrested</u> for <u>failing</u> to "update" his sex offender registration between July 17th and July 22nd, as the registration statute <u>requires</u>. The registration statute <u>makes</u> failure to update an independent felony.

6. At his trial before a judge, Blanchard's counsel argued that Blanchard did not need to "update" his registration, because nothing had changed in the few days since his registration on July 15th. The trial judge rejected that argument and found Blanchard guilty.

7. Our state's so-called "Three Strikes" law permits a person to be sentenced from 25 years to life for a third felony, and the trial judge sentenced Blanchard to 40 years in state prison. On this appeal, we must decide whether that sentence is so disproportionate to the gravity of Blanchard's offense as to constitute cruel or unusual punishment in violation of the Eighth Amendment or its counterpart in our state constitution.

The Passive Can Create Ambiguity

The passive voice takes more words than the active voice, but that is not its only disadvantage. The passive voice can be ambiguous. With the active voice, you can usually tell who is doing what to whom. With the passive voice, however, the writer can hide the identity of the actor. That construction is called the "truncated passive." For example: "The ball was kicked." Who kicked the ball? We have no way to know; the actor is hidden in the fog of the truncated passive. Bureaucrats love to write in the truncated passive because it lets them hide in the fog; the reader cannot discover who is responsible for the action (or the lack of it).

A writer who wants to befog the matter totally will couple the truncated passive with a nominalization, like this: "A kicking action was accomplished," thus hiding both the kicker and the kickee. The truncated passive can be especially troublesome in legal writing. Consider this patent license provision:

> All improvements of the patented invention that are made hereafter shall promptly be disclosed, and failure to do so shall be deemed a material breach of this license agreement.

Who must disclose improvements to whom? Must the licensor disclose improvements it makes to the licensee? Must the licensee disclose improvements it makes to the licensor? Must each party disclose improvements it makes to the other party? If it ever becomes important to know, the parties will probably have to slug it out in a lawsuit, all because of the truncated passive voice.

Notice that the title of this chapter says *prefer* the active voice. It *doesn't* say never use the passive voice. The passive voice has many proper uses. For instance, you can use it when the thing done is important, and who did it is not:

> The subpoena was served on January 19th.

Or you can use it when you don't know who did it:

> The data files were mysteriously destroyed.

Or you can use it when you want the subject of the sentence to connect with words at the end of the preceding sentence:

> The committee presented the award to Frederick Moore. Moore was arrested by the FBI the following day.

Or you can use it to place a strong element at the end of the sentence for emphasis:

> When he walked through the door, the victim was shot.

Or you can use it when a sense of detached abstraction is appropriate:

> In the eyes of the law, all persons are created equal.

Or you can use it when you want to muddy the waters. For example, if you do not want to state outright that your client knocked out the plaintiff's teeth, you can say:

The plaintiff's teeth were knocked out.

Thus, if you can articulate a good reason for using the passive voice, then use it. But elsewhere, use the active voice; it will make your writing clearer and more concise.

↶ Exercise 8

Rewrite these sentences, omitting surplus words and using the active voice unless you can articulate a good reason for using the passive voice. Supply any missing information that you need. Then look at the exercise key in the Appendix.

- 1. Trading in the defendant corporation's stock was suspended by the stock exchange at 10:17 the following morning.

- 2. The bank was not notified by either the depositor or anyone else that the ATM card had been stolen.

- 3. Dept. of Agriculture Form 9-2018 must be filled in and brought to any USDA branch office before any genetically modified sugar beet seed can be planted in an open field.

- 4. After 180 days, this Agreement can be terminated by either party.

- 5. Two kilograms of an unidentified white powder were discovered in the spare tire well of defendant's Volvo sedan.

- 6. Charitable gifts of appreciated assets can be deducted at their fair market value at the time of the gift, and in that way capital gains tax can be avoided.

Chapter 5

Use Short Sentences

For centuries, English-speaking lawyers have been addicted to long, complicated sentences. The long sentence habit began back when English writers used punctuation to guide oral delivery, rather than to help convey the meaning of a sentence.[1] In law, the long sentence habit persisted even after orderly division of thought had become routine in ordinary English prose. When lawyers write, they tend to deliver to the reader in one fat lump all their main themes, supporting reasons, details, qualifications, exceptions, and conclusions. In particular, statutes and regulations grind on, line after line, perhaps on the theory that if the readers come to a period they will rush out to violate the law without bothering to read to the end. Consider this wire-tapping statute:

Any person who, by means of any machine, instrument, or contrivance, or in any other manner, intentionally taps, or makes any unauthorized connection, whether physically, electrically, acoustically, inductively, or otherwise, with any telegraph or telephone wire, line, cable, or instrument of any internal telephonic communications system, or who willfully and without consent of all parties to the communication, or in an unauthorized manner, reads, or attempts to read, or to learn the contents or meaning of any message, report, or communication while the same is in transit or passing over any wire, line or cable, or is being sent from or received at any place within this state; or who uses, or attempts to use, in any manner, or for any purpose, or to communicate in any way, any information so obtained, or who aids, agrees with, employs, or conspires with any person or persons to unlawfully do, or permit, or cause to be done any of the acts or things mentioned above in this section, is punishable by a fine not exceeding two thousand five hundred dollars ($2,500), or by imprisonment in the county jail not exceeding one year, or by imprisonment in the state prison not exceeding three years, or by both such fine and imprisonment in the county jail or in the state prison.[2]

That sentence contains 217 words and no fewer than eighteen separate thoughts. No wonder it is hard to swallow.

Long sentences make legal writing hard to understand. To prove this to yourself, read the following passage at your normal speed. Then ask yourself what it means.

In a trial by jury, the court may, when the convenience of witnesses or the ends of justice would be promoted thereby, on motion of a party, after notice and hearing, make an order, no later than the close of the pretrial conference in cases in which such pretrial conference is to be held, or in other cases, no later than 10 days before the trial date, that the trial of the issue of liability shall precede the trial of any other issue in the case.

The subject matter of that passage is not profound or complicated, but the passage is hard to understand. It consists of a single sentence, 86 words long, containing five pieces of information:

1. In a jury case, the liability issue may be tried before any other issue.

2. The judge may order the liability issue to be tried first if that will serve the convenience of witnesses or the ends of justice.

3. The judge may make the order on a party's motion, after notice and hearing.

4. In a case with a pretrial conference, the judge may make the order no later than the end of the conference.

5. In a case with no pretrial conference, the judge may make the order no later than ten days before the trial date.

The original passage is hard to understand for two reasons. First, the single-sentence format caused the author to distort the logical order of the five pieces of information. The first thing the readers want to know is what the passage is about. It is about the trial of the liability issue before other issues. But before the readers discover that, they must climb through a thicket of subsidiary ideas and arrive at the last twenty words of the sentence.

Second, the single-sentence format strains a reader's memory. The subject of the sentence (*court*) appears at word seven. At word 32, the verb (*make*) finally shows up. Part of the object (*an order*) comes next, but the critical part remains hidden until the reader arrives, breathless, at word 68. By then the reader has forgotten the subject and verb and must search back in the sentence to find them.

The remedy for such a passage is simple. Instead of one long sentence containing five thoughts, use five sentences, each containing one thought. Here is one way the passage could be rewritten:

In a jury case, the court may order the liability issue to be tried before any other issue. The court may make such an order if doing so serves the convenience of witnesses or the ends of justice. The court may make the order on a party's motion, after notice and hearing. In a case with a pretrial conference, the court may make the order no later than the end of the conference. In a case with no pretrial conference, the court may make the order no later than ten days before the trial date.

Instead of one 86 word sentence, we now have five sentences with an average length of 19 words. Each sentence contains only one main thought, and the thoughts follow in logical sequence. Passages like the one above suggest a two-part guide to clarity and ease of understanding in legal writing:

1. In *most* sentences, put only one main thought.
2. Keep the *average* sentence length below 25 words.[3]

Do not misinterpret this guide. Part 1 says that *most* sentences should contain only one main thought. It does *not* say that *every* sentence should contain only one main thought. To keep the reader's interest, you need variety in sentence construction: some simple sentences that express only one main thought, interspersed with some compound or complex sentences that express two or more related thoughts.

Likewise, Part 2 says that the *average* length of your sentences should be below twenty-five words. It does *not* say that *every* sentence should be twenty-five words or less. You need variety in sentence length as well as sentence construction: some short sentences, some of medium length, and an occasional long one in which related thoughts are joined.

When you write a long sentence, however, bear in mind Mark Twain's advice. After recommending short sentences as the general rule, he added:

> At times [the writer] may indulge himself with a long one, but he will make sure there are no folds in it, no vaguenesses, no parenthetical interruptions of its view as a whole; when he has done with it, it won't be a sea-serpent with half of its arches under the water; it will be a torchlight procession.[4]

❧ Exercise 9

Rewrite these passages using short sentences and omitting as many surplus words as you can. Then look at the exercise key in the Appendix.

1. In an action grounded upon the law of torts, an actor is not liable for harm that is different from the harms whose risks made the actor's conduct tortious, nor for harm when the tortious aspect of the actor's conduct did not increase the risk of harm, but when an actor's tortious conduct causes harm to a person that, because of the person's preexisting physical or mental condition or other characteristic, is of a greater magnitude or different type than might reasonably be expected, the actor is nevertheless liable for all such harm to the person. (96 words, average sentence length 96 words)

2. In decisions concerning the sentencing and correction of individual offenders, the general purposes of the law ought to be to render punishment within a range of severity sufficient to reflect the gravity of the offense and blameworthiness of the offenders, and where there is a realistic prospect of success, to serve the goals of offender rehabilitation, general deterrence, incapacitation of dangerous offenders, and restoration of crime victims and communities, but to impose sentences no more severe than necessary to achieve the foregoing purposes. (83 words, average sentence length 83 words)

3. Under the law of "gifts to a class of people," if in vitro fertilization is used by a husband and wife to produce a pregnancy in the wife, the sperm sometimes comes from the husband and sometimes from a third party, just as the eggs sometimes come from the wife and sometimes from a third party. A

child produced from the husband's sperm and the wife's eggs is the genetic child of the husband and wife and is so treated for class-gift purposes, but if a child is produced from a third party's sperm or a third party's eggs, with the embryo being placed in the uterus of the wife to cause the pregnancy, then the child is the genetic child of the sperm or egg donor, yet for class-gift purposes that child is treated as the child of the husband and wife, not as the child of a third-party sperm or egg donor. (154 words, average sentence length 77 words)

Notes

1. The history of the long, long sentence is told in David Mellinkoff, *The Language of the Law* 152–70 (Little, Brown 1963); *see also* Peter M. Tiersma, *Legal Language* 55–59 (Chicago 1999); David Mellinkoff, *Legal Writing: Sense & Nonsense* 58–60 (West 1982).

2. Cal. Pen. Code §631(a) (West 1999).

3. Your computer's word processing program can count words and compute words per sentence in a flash. In the WordPerfect program I use, I just click File, then Properties, then Information. If you want to do it the old-fashioned way, pick a paragraph or two and count the number of words from one period to the next. Count hyphenated words and groups of symbols as one word. Do not count legal citations. For example, this sentence would be counted as 20 words:

    1   2   3   4   5   6   7
The twin-drive concept was obvious from IBM's

  8   9   10 11   12   13
'497 patent; under the Graham test, 382 U.S.

           14 15 16   17   18   19 20
at 17–18, that is enough to invalidate Claim 12.

When you measure a sentence that includes a tabulated list (see chapter 6, below), treat the initial colon and the semicolons as periods.

4. As quoted in Ernest Gowers, *The Complete Plain Words* 166–67 (1st U.S. ed., revised by Sidney Greenbaum and Janet Whitcut, published by David R. Godine 1988). Sir Ernest footnotes the Twain quotation to John Earle, *English Prose: Its Elements, History, and Usage* 517–18 (Smith, Elder & Co., London 1890). Earle was the Rawlinsonian Professor of Anglo-Saxon at Oxford, and he found the

quotation in a collection of letters from well-known writers of the late 1800s. The letters were solicited and assembled by another Englishman, George Bainton, in a volume designed to teach aspiring writers the craft of good writing. *See* George Bainton, *The Art of Authorship: Literary Reminiscences, Methods of Work, and Advice to Young Beginners* 87 (James Clarke & Co., London 1890).

Chapter 6

Arrange Your Words with Care

Avoid Wide Gaps Between the Subject, the Verb, and the Object

To make your writing easy to understand, most of your declaratory sentences should follow the normal English word order: first the subject, next the verb, and then the object (if there is one). For example:

> <u>subject</u>   <u>verb</u>
> The <u>defendant</u> <u>demurred</u>.

> <u>subject</u>   <u>verb</u>   <u>object</u>
> The <u>defendant</u> <u>filed</u> six <u>affidavits</u>.

In seeking to understand a sentence, the reader's mind searches for the subject, the verb, and the object. If those three key elements are set out in that order, close together, near the front of the sentence, then the reader will understand quickly.

Lawyers, however, like to test the agility of their readers by making them leap wide gaps between the subject and the verb and between the verb and the object. For example:

> A claim, which in the case of negligent misconduct shall not exceed $500, and in the case of intentional misconduct shall not exceed $1,000, may be filed with the Office of the Administrator by any injured party.

In that sentence, the reader must leap a twenty-two word gap to get from the subject (claim) to the verb (may be filed). The best remedy for a gap that wide is to turn the intervening words into a separate sentence:

> Any injured party may file a claim with the Office of the Administrator. A claim must not exceed $500 for negligent misconduct, or $1,000 for intentional misconduct.

Smaller gaps between subject and verb can be closed by moving the intervening words to the beginning or the end of the sentence:

Gap	Gap Closed
This agreement, unless revocation has occurred at an earlier date, shall expire on November 1, 2012.	Unless sooner revoked, this agreement expires on November 1, 2012.
The defendant, in addition to having to pay punitive damages, may be liable for plaintiff's costs and attorney fees.	The defendant may have to pay plaintiff's costs and attorney fees in addition to punitive damages.

The problem is the same when the gap comes between the verb and the object:

> The proposed statute gives to any person who suffers financial injury by reason of discrimination based on race, religion, sex, or physical handicap a cause of action for treble damages.

Here a twenty-one word gap comes between the verb (gives) and the direct object (cause of action). One remedy is to make two sentences. Another is to move the intervening words to the end of the sentence:

> The proposed statute gives a cause of action for treble damages to any person who suffers financial injury because of

discrimination based on race, religion, sex, or physical handicap.

∾ Exercise 10

Revise these sentences, putting the subject, verb, and object(s) close together and near the front of the sentence, and omitting as many surplus words as you can. Then look at the exercise key in the Appendix.

1. A building contractor, after complying with a property owner's request to make a significant deviation from the plans and specifications previously agreed upon, may impose a reasonable additional charge for the deviation.

2. A lawyer, having offered her client's testimony in the belief that it was true, and having subsequently come to know that the evidence is false, must take "reasonable remedial measures."

3. "Reasonable remedial measures," as used in the *Restatement (Third) of the Law Governing Lawyers* § 120 (2000) and American Bar Association Model Code of Professional Responsibility, Rule 3.3, includes as a first step remonstrating with the client in confidence, telling the client about the lawyer's duty of candor to the tribunal, and seeking the client's cooperation with respect to the withdrawal or correction of the false testimony.

4. The second remedial step, which should be taken if and only if there is a failure of the first step, described above, is for the lawyer, always seeking to cause the minimum amount of harm to the client and the client's legitimate objectives, to consider withdrawing from the representation, if withdrawal will undo the effects of the false evidence.

5. Disclosure of the falsehood to the tribunal, which is the third and ultimate remedial step and which is to be taken only after

it becomes apparent that the first two steps are unavailing, is a drastic step in that the lawyer is allowed, in situations where it is necessary, to reveal information to the tribunal that would otherwise be protected by the attorney-client privilege and/or the ethical duty of confidentiality.

Put Conditions and Exceptions Where They Are Clear and Easy to Read

When lawyers draft contracts, statutes, rules, and the like, they often use conditions (if A and B, then C) and exceptions (D, except when E or F). One can imagine a language with strict rules about where in a sentence to put conditions and exceptions—for example, a rule that conditions always go at the beginning of the sentence and exceptions always go at the end. The English language has no such rules, so the writer must decide, sentence by sentence, where to put conditions and exceptions, guided by the need for clarity and readability.[1] Usually, the *end* of the sentence is the best place for a condition or exception that is longer than the main clause. For example:

> A lawyer may disclose a client's confidential information *if disclosure is necessary to prevent, mitigate, or rectify substantial injury to the financial interests or property of another that is reasonably certain to result or has resulted from the client's commission of a crime or fraud in furtherance of which the client has used the lawyer's services.*

Conversely, the *beginning* of the sentence is usually the best place if the condition or exception is short, or if it needs to be at the beginning to avoid leading the reader astray. For example:

> *Except for U.S. citizens,* all persons passing this point must have in their possession a valid passport, a baggage clearance certificate, and a yellow entry card.

When Necessary, Make a List

Sometimes the best way to present a cluster of conditions, or exceptions, or other closely related ideas is with an introductory clause followed by a list.[2] Here is a sentence that needs the list trick:

> You can qualify for benefits under Section 43 if you are sixty-four or older and unable to work, and that section also provides benefits in the event that you are blind in one eye, or both eyes, or are permanently disabled in the course of your employment.

The list trick transforms the sentence to this:

> You can qualify for benefits under Section 43 if you meet any one of the following conditions:
> - you are 64 or older and are unable to work; or
> - you are blind in one or both eyes; or
> - you are permanently disabled in the course of your employment.

When you use the list trick, follow these conventions:

1. The items in the list must be parallel in substance. Don't make a list like this:
   a. bread;
   b. eggs; and
   c. Czar Nicholas II.

2. The items in the list must be parallel in grammar. Don't make a list like this:
   a. jurisdiction;
   b. venue; and
   c. preparing charts for Dr. Sullivan's testimony.

3. After each item in the list, except the last, put a semicolon followed by *or* (if the list is disjunctive) or *and* (if the list

is conjunctive). If both the list and the items are short, and if the reader will not become confused, you can omit the *and* or *or* after all except the next-to-last item. Also, you don't need *and* or *or* if the list is neither conjunctive nor disjunctive.

4. Put the list at the end of the passage, not at the beginning and not in the middle.[3]

5. In a complicated drafting task, you may find that an item in a list is complex enough to require a list of its own. You can create a list within a list, but avoid more than two ranks of lists[4] (unless you admire the Internal Revenue Code).[5]

As you can see from the foregoing paragraph, you can also use a list to bring order to a series of related, complete sentences.

℃ Exercise 11

Revise the following passage, omitting surplus words and using the list trick where appropriate. Then look at the exercise key in the Appendix.

Provided that it does not exceed the limitations imposed by its charter, or by the laws of the sovereign State of South Carolina, or by the laws of the United States of America, or by the Constitution of the United States of America, or by the Constitution of the sovereign State of South Carolina, a home owners' association chartered by the sovereign State of South Carolina has the implied power to make reasonable rules and regulations concerning use of the common property of the association's members, and governing the use of the members' individual property to protect the common property. In addition to this implied power, an association's charter may give it a general power to adopt reasonable rules and regulations designed for the protec-

tion of members' individually owned property from unreasonable interference caused by other members' use of either the common property or the other members' individually owned property.

Put Modifying Words Close to What They Modify

In some languages, the order of words within a sentence does not
affect the meaning of the sentence. But in English, word order does
affect meaning, as this sentence shows:

The defendant was arrested for fornicating under a little-
used state statute.

Modifying words tend to do their work on whatever you put
them near. Therefore, as a general rule, put modifying words as
close as you can to the words you want them to modify. That will
help avoid sentences like these:

My client has discussed your proposal to fill the drainage
ditch with his partners.

Being beyond any doubt insane, Judge Weldon ordered the
petitioner's transfer to a state mental hospital.

Beware of the "squinting" modifier—one that sits mid-sentence
and can be read to modify either what precedes it or what follows
it:

A trustee who steals dividends often cannot be punished.

What does *often* modify? Does the sentence tell us that crime frequently pays? Or that frequent crime pays?

Once discovered, a squinting modifier is easy to cure. Either
choose a word that does not squint, or rearrange the sentence to
avoid the ambiguity. For example:

When workers are injured frequently no compensation is paid.

If that means that injured workers frequently receive no compensation, the squinting modifier could be moved to the front of the sentence, like this:

Frequently, workers who are injured receive no compensation.

The word *only* is a notorious troublemaker. For example, in the following sentence the word *only* could go in any of seven places and produce a half a dozen different meanings:

She said that he shot her.

To keep *only* under control, put it immediately before the word you want it to modify. If it creates ambiguity in that position, try to isolate it at the beginning or ending of the sentence:

Ambiguous	Clear
Lessee shall use the vessel only for recreation.	Lessee must use the vessel for recreation only.
Shares are sold to the public only by the parent corporation.	Only the parent corporation sells shares to the public.

Watch out for ambiguity in sentences like this one:

The grantor was Maxwell Aaron, the father of Sarah Aaron, who later married Pat Snyder.

Who married Pat—Maxwell or Sarah? Some lawyers try to clear up this kind of ambiguity by piling on more words:

The grantor was Maxwell Aaron, father of Sarah Aaron, which said Maxwell Aaron later married Pat Snyder.

But it's easier than that. You can usually avoid ambiguity by placing the relative pronoun (like *who, which,* and *that*) right after the word to which it relates. If Pat's spouse were Maxwell, the sentence could be rearranged to read:

> The grantor was Sarah Aaron's father, Maxwell Aaron, who later married Pat Snyder.

Sometimes a relative pronoun will not behave, no matter where you put it:

> Claims for expenses, which must not exceed $100, must be made within 30 days.

What must not exceed $100—the claims or the expenses? Here the best remedy is simply to omit the relative pronoun:

> Claims for expenses must not exceed $100 and must be made within 30 days.

or

> Expenses must not exceed $100. Claims for expenses must be made within 30 days.

℃ Exercise 12

Revise these sentences to solve the modifier problems. If a sentence has more than one possible meaning, select whichever one you wish and revise the sentence to express that meaning unambiguously. Then look at the exercise key in the Appendix.

1. The airline's mechanics only said that the fuel tank had been repaired.

2. Being fearful for her life, counsel argued that the defendant acted in self-defense.

3. Appellant's brief fails to consider the changes to the pension provisions that were adopted in 2005.

4. Patently lacking any kind of consideration, the trial judge held that the contract was void.

5. The new dairy regulations were intended to reduce the open-air discharge of methane gas by the Department of Agriculture.

Avoid Nested Modifiers

When I was a child, one of my favorite toys was a figure carved from smooth dark wood, the figure of a seated, round Navajo woman. She came apart in the middle to reveal an identical but smaller woman inside. The second woman likewise came apart to reveal a third, and the third a fourth.

Perverse lawyers write sentences that are constructed like my Navajo women. For example:

Defendant, who was driving a flatbed truck that was laden with a tangle of old furniture some of which was not tied down securely, stopped without warning.

Here is the same sentence written with brackets and parentheses:

Defendant {who was driving a flatbed truck [that was laden with a tangle of old furniture (some of which was not tied down securely)]} stopped without warning.

That sentence is like my Navajo women because it contains a set of modifying phrases, each nested inside the next. The sentence is hard to understand because the reader must mentally supply brackets and parentheses to keep the modifiers straight.

The best remedy for such a sentence is to take apart the nest of modifiers and put some of the information in a separate sentence. Consider this passage for example:

A claim for exemption, which in the case of a dwelling that is used for housing not more than a single family shall not exceed $300,000 or the fair market value, whichever is less, may be filed with the Administrator within 90 days after receipt of notice.

When broken in two, the passage reads like this:

A claim for exemption may be filed with the Administrator within 90 days after receipt of notice. The claim for a single family dwelling cannot exceed $300,000, or the fair market value, whichever is less.

❧ Exercise 13

Revise these sentences, omitting surplus words and untangling nested modifiers. Then see the exercise key in the Appendix.

1. Conflicts of interest, which can seriously erode, if not destroy entirely, the relationship of trust between attorney and client, are generally imputed to all attorneys in the firm.

2. One type of conflict of interest, in which an attorney enters into a business transaction of whatever kind, even a transaction that produces handsome profits for all concerned, with a client, can be solved if the attorney makes sure that four conditions are satisfied.

3. One of the four conditions is that the terms of the transaction, which must be fair and reasonable to the client, must be disclosed, in a writing that uses clear, plain language, to the client.

Clarify the Reach of Modifiers

Suppose that the owner of a pet store agrees to sell part of her stock to someone else. The contract of sale states that it covers "all female rabbits and hamsters over six-weeks-old." The contract is ambiguous, and the ambiguity is caused by the uncertain reach of the two modifiers *female* and *over six-weeks-old*. We can't tell whether *female* stops with *rabbits*, or whether it reaches forward to *hamsters* as well. Further, we can't tell whether *over six-weeks-old* stops with *hamsters*, or whether it reaches backward to *rabbits* as well. Thus, the contract may cover any of four combinations:

1. [all female rabbits, however old] + [all hamsters over six-weeks-old, of whatever sex]; or

2. [all female rabbits, however old] + [all female hamsters over six-weeks-old]; or

3. [all female rabbits over six-weeks-old] + [all hamsters over six-weeks-old, of whatever sex]; or

4. [all female rabbits over six-weeks-old] + [all female hamsters over six-weeks-old].

To avoid this kind of ambiguity, you must clarify the reach of the modifiers in your sentences. Sometimes you can do that simply by changing the word order:

Ambiguous	Clear
women and men over 30	men over 30 and women
alto saxophones and bassoons	bassoons and alto saxophones

Other times, you can clarify the reach of a modifier by repeating words or making a list.

Ambiguous	Clear
endangered frogs and salamanders	endangered frogs and endangered salamanders
all vans, sport utility vehicles, autos, and trucks without four-wheel drive	all vehicles without four-wheel drive, including vans, sport utility vehicles, autos, and trucks

∾ Exercise 14

Clarify the reach of the modifiers in these sentences. If a sentence has more than one possible meaning, select whichever one you wish and revise the sentence to express that meaning unambiguously. Then look at the exercise key in the Appendix.

1. An attorney is allowed to reveal a client's confidential information to prevent death, serious bodily injury, or serious financial injury due to a crime the client is about to commit.

2. A witness's prior criminal conviction can be used for impeachment if it was a felony or misdemeanor involving dishonesty or false statement.

3. A corporation is liable for financial losses suffered by an investor due to criminal conduct of a high-ranking officer or employee acting within the scope of his or her authority.

Notes

1. For more specific guidance, *see* Bryan A. Garner, *Guidelines for Drafting and Editing Court Rules*, 169 F.R.D. 177, 190–94 (1997).

2. *See* Reed Dickerson, *The Fundamentals of Legal Drafting* 115–24 (2nd ed. Little, Brown 1986).

3. According to British Commonwealth drafting expert Garth Thornton, a list sitting mid-sentence becomes a list sandwich. *See* G.C. Thornton, *Legislative Drafting* 63 (4th ed. Butterworths 1996); *see also* Bryan A. Garner, *Legal Writing in Plain English* 100–104 (Chicago 2001).

4. Reed Dickerson suggested a maximum of three (rather than two) ranks of lists, but even he counseled moderation in using the list trick. Dickerson, *The Fundamentals of Legal Drafting* 118.

5. For an example of too many ranks of lists, *see* 26 U.S.C. §167 (2000), concerning depreciation for federal income tax purposes.

Chapter 7

Choose Your Words with Care

Here are two ways a lawyer might begin a letter to a client to explain why the lawyer's bill is higher than the client expected:

Example One

The statement for professional services that you will find enclosed herewith is, in all likelihood, somewhat in excess of your expectations. In the circumstances, I believe it is incumbent upon me to avail myself of this opportunity to provide you with an explanation of the causes therefor. It is my considered judgment that three factors are responsible for this development.

Example Two

The bill I am sending you with this letter is probably higher than you expected, and I would like to explain the three reasons why.

Example One is awful, is it not? It contains many of the faults we have already discussed—a flock of nominalizations, for example. But notice also the choice of words in Example One. Why does its author say *statement for professional services* instead of *bill*? The client calls it a bill. So does the lawyer, usually. By tradition, the bill itself can be captioned *statement for professional services*. But this is supposed to be a friendly, candid letter to a client; let us call a bill a *bill*.

Why does the author of Example One use *herewith* and *therefor*? To give the letter the scent of old law books? Why does the author use airy, abstract words like *circumstances, factors,* and *development*? Do they somehow add dignity? Finally, why does the author use ponderous phrases instead of the simple words used in Example Two:

Example One	Example Two
in all likelihood	probably
in excess of your expectations	higher than you expected
explanation of the causes	explain why

Use Concrete Words

To grip and move your reader's mind, use concrete words, not abstractions. For example, here is how Exodus 7:20–21 describes Moses inflicting a plague on Egypt:

> He lifted up the rod and smote the waters of the river … and all the waters that were in the river were turned to blood. And the fish that were in the river died; and the river stank, and the Egyptians could not drink the water of the river; and there was blood throughout all the land of Egypt.

Now suppose that same event were described in the language of a modern environmental impact report:

> The water was impacted by his rod, whereupon a polluting effect was achieved. The consequent toxification reduced the conditions necessary for the sustenance of the indigenous population of aquatic vertebrates below the level of viability. Olfactory discomfort standards were substantially exceeded, and potability declined. Social, economic, and political disorientation were experienced to an unprecedented degree.

The lure of abstract words is strong for lawyers. Lawyers want to be cautious and to cover every possibility, while leaving room to wiggle out if necessary. The vagueness of abstract words therefore seems attractive. Particularly attractive are words like *basis, situation, consideration, facet, character, factor, degree, aspect* and *circumstances:*[1]

> In our present circumstances, the budgetary aspect is a factor which must be taken into consideration to a greater degree.

Perhaps that means "now we must think more about money," but the meaning is a shadow in the fog of abstract words.

Do not mistake abstraction of that sort for the intentional, artful vagueness sometimes required in legal writing. For example, judicial opinions sometimes use an intentionally vague phrase to provide a general compass heading when it is not possible to map the trail in detail. In *Bates v. State Bar of Arizona,*[2] the Supreme Court announced that lawyer advertising is protected under the First Amendment commercial speech doctrine. The Court wanted to tell the states that they could regulate truthful lawyer advertising *some,* but not too much. The Court could not then tell how much would be too much, so it said that states may impose "*reasonable restrictions*" on the time, place and manner of lawyer advertising.[3] The phrase was intentionally vague. It gave general guidance, but it postponed specific guidance until specific facts were presented to the Court in later cases.

Intentional vagueness is likewise used in drafting statutes, contracts, and the like, when the drafter cannot foresee every set of facts that may arise. But vagueness is a virtue only if it is both necessary and intentional. Knowing when to be vague and when to press for more concrete terms is part of the art of lawyering.

Use Familiar Words

Aristotle put the case for familiar words this way: "Style to be good must be clear.... Speech which fails to convey a plain meaning will fail to do just what speech has to do.... Clearness is secured by using the words ... that are current and ordinary."[4] Given a choice between a familiar word and one that will send your reader groping for the dictionary, use the familiar word. The reader's attention is a precious commodity, and you cannot afford to waste it by creating distractions.

Unlike many writers, attorneys usually know who their readers will be, and their choice of words can be tailored accordingly. A patent lawyer who is writing a brief to be filed in the United States Court of Appeals for the Federal Circuit can use legal terms that might be perplexing if used in a letter to the lawyer's inventor-client. Conversely, in writing to the inventor-client, the patent lawyer can use scientific terms that would be hypertechnical if used in a legal brief. In either case, the convenience of the reader must take precedence over the self-gratification of the writer.

Even among familiar words, prefer the simple to the stuffy. Don't say *termination* if *end* will do as well. Don't use *expedite* for hurry, or *elucidate* for explain, or *utilize* for use. Do not conclude that your vocabulary should shrink to preschool size. If an unfamiliar word is fresh and fits your need better than any other, use it—but don't *utilize* it.

Do Not Use Lawyerisms

Lawyerisms are words like *aforementioned, whereas, res gestae,* and *hereinafter*. They give writing a legal smell, but they carry little or no legal substance. When they are used in writing addressed to non-lawyers, they baffle and annoy. When used in other legal writing, they give a false sense of precision and sometimes obscure a dangerous gap in analysis.

A lawyer's words should not differ without reason from the words used in ordinary English. Sometimes there is a reason. For example, the Latin phrase *res ipsa loquitur* has become a term of art[5] that lawyers use to communicate among themselves, conveniently and with a fair degree of precision, about a tort law doctrine.[6] But too often lawyers use Latin or archaic English phrases needlessly. Sometimes they do it out of habit or haste; the old phrase is the one they learned in law school, and they have never taken time to question its use. Other times they do it believing mistakenly that the old phrase's meaning cannot be expressed in ordinary English, or that the old phrase is somehow more precise than ordinary English.

Consider, for example, the word *said* in its archaic use as an adjective. No lawyer in dinner table conversation says: "The green beans are excellent; please pass said green beans." Yet legal pleadings come out like this:

> The object of said conspiracy among said defendants was to fix said retail prices of said products in interstate commerce.

Lawyers who use *said* claim that it is more precise than ordinary words like *the,* or *this,* or *those.* They say it means "the exact same one mentioned above." But the extra precision is either illusory or unnecessary, as the above example shows. If only one conspiracy has been mentioned in the preceding material, we will not mistake *this* conspiracy for some other conspiracy, and *said* is unnecessary. If more than one conspiracy has been previously mentioned, *said* does not tell us which of the several is meant. The extra precision is thus illusory. If *the* were put in place of all the *saids*, the sentence would be no less precise and much less clumsy.

Aforementioned is *said*'s big brother, and it is just as useless. "The fifty-acre plot aforementioned shall be divided...." If only one fifty-acre plot has been mentioned before, then *aforementioned* is unnecessary, and if more than one fifty-acre plot has been mentioned before, then *aforementioned* is imprecise. When precision is important, use a specific reference: "The fifty-acre plot described in paragraph 2(f) shall be divided ...."

Res gestae is an example of a Latin lawyerism that can obscure a dangerous gap in analysis. Translated, it means "things done." In the early 1800s, it was used to denote statements that were made as part of the transaction in issue (the "things done") and that were therefore admissible in evidence over hearsay objection. Perhaps because *res gestae* is far removed from ordinary English, lawyers and judges began to treat it as a ragbag. They used it carelessly to cover many different kinds of statements made at or about the time of the transaction in issue.[7] With policy and analysis obscured, *res gestae* became little more than a label to express the conclusion that a particular statement ought to be admitted into evidence over hearsay objection. Wigmore said: "The phrase 'res gestae' has long been not only entirely useless, but even positively harmful.... It is harmful, because by its ambiguity it invites the confusion of one rule with another and thus creates uncertainty as to the limitations of both."[8]

The moral is this: do not be too impressed by the Latin and archaic English words you read in law books. Their antiquity does not make them superior. When your pen is poised to write a lawyerism, stop to see if your meaning can be expressed as well or better in a word or two of ordinary English.

ᑳ Exercise 15

Revise the following sentences, omitting surplus words and using familiar, concrete words where you can. Then look at the exercise key in the Appendix.

1. In *Simpson v. Union Oil Co.*, Justice William O. Douglas announced, *ipse dixit*: "The patent laws which give a seventeen-year monopoly on 'making, using, or selling the invention' are *in pari materia* with the antitrust laws and modify them *pro tanto*. That was the *ratio decidendi* of the *General Electric* case."

2. Effectuation of improvement in the efficiency of the microlending market in the nations of Central America is dependent in part upon the creation of innovative methods of

sharing loan default data among lenders without incentiviz-ing them to engage in non-competitive collaboration *inter se* on interest rates and risk assessment.

3. Appearances then were duly entered, Cecil Wickham, Q.C., *pro querente,* and defendant Augustine Crump *in propria per-sona.*

Avoid Shotgunning

When we lawyers want to be precise and cover every possibility, we too often use the shotgun approach—we take rough aim and loose a blast of words, hoping that at least one of them might hit the target. Consider, for example, this criminal statute:

> Every person who ... overdrives, overloads, drives when overloaded, overworks, tortures, torments, deprives of nec-essary sustenance, drink, or shelter, cruelly beats, mutilates, or cruelly kills any animal, or causes or procures any ani-mal to be so overdriven, overloaded, overworked, tortured, tormented, deprived of necessary sustenance, drink or shel-ter, or to be cruelly beaten, mutilated, or cruelly killed ... is guilty of a crime....[9]

The simplest remedy for shotgunning is to search your mind for a single word that will adequately express the intended meaning. In the statute above, the single verb *"abuse"* could replace the ten-verb shotgun blast.

Sometimes the simple remedy will not suffice. For instance, the author of the animal abuse statute may have feared that a judge would find the single verb *"abuse"* too vague to give the public fair notice of the kinds of conduct covered by the statute. Where vagueness poses a problem, the best course is to choose a serviceable term and define it for the reader.[10] Then, use the term consistently throughout the document, being cautious not to depart from its defined meaning.

In Rule Drafting, Prefer the Singular Number and the Present Tense

When you draft a statute, regulation, bylaw, or other document that states rules, and you have a choice between the singular and the plural, use the singular unless you can articulate a sound reason for using the plural.[11]

Do This	Not This
A person must not discharge a firearm inside city limits.	Persons must not discharge firearms inside city limits.

The most common reason for using the plural is to refer to a group of people rather than to individuals within the group. For example:

Group—Use Plural

The Admissions Director will identify applicants whose college grades indicate high achievement despite adversity.

Individual within a Group—Use Singular

When the Director identifies an applicant whose college grades indicate high achievement despite adversity, the Director will flag that applicant's file.

Similarly, in rule drafting, use the present tense unless you can articulate a sound reason for using the past, future, or other tense.[12]

Do This	Not This
If a voter *spoils* his or her ballot ...	If a voter *shall spoil* his or her ballot ...
A person who *sells* liquor within two miles of a college or university ...	A person who *has sold* liquor within two miles of a college or university ...

If contrary information	If contrary information *has*
becomes available, a sup-	*become* available, a supple-
plemental response *is*	mental response *will be*
required.	required.

One reason for using something other than the present tense is to set up a time relationship in the rule. For example, use the appropriate tense for an event that preceded the rule, or an event that will necessarily happen before or after the event you are describing in the rule:

> A member of the armed forces who *was stationed* in Iraq after January 1, 2004, but who *did not receive* combat pay, is eligible ...

> If a jurisdiction *has adopted* a graffiti abatement program as defined in subsection (f), the court may order the defendant to clean up ...

> No interest in property is valid unless it *will vest*, if at all, within 21 years after a life in being at the creation of the interest ...

Use Words of Authority with Care

When you draft rules, contracts, and other formal legal documents, be precise and consistent in using words of authority such as *must, shall, will, may, should* and their negative forms, such as *must not,* and *will not.*[13] The biggest troublemaker is *shall.* Sometimes lawyers use it to impose a duty: "The defendant *shall* file an answer within 30 days ..." Other times lawyers use it to express a future action ("the lease shall terminate ...") or even an entitlement ("the landlord shall have the right to inspect ...") Drafting experts have identified several additional shades of meaning *shall* can carry.[14] To make matters worse, many lawyers do not realize how slippery *shall* is, so they use it freely, unaware of the booby traps it creates.

The legislative drafters in some jurisdictions in the United States try to tame *shall* by using it only in its command sense: *shall* imposes a duty to do something.[15] In recent years, however, many U.S. drafting authorities have come around to the British Commonwealth view: don't use *shall* for any purpose—it is simply too unreliable.[16]

Throwing out *shall* leaves us with a fairly well-behaved roster of words to express duty, permission, discretion, entitlement, and the like. These words should be used consistently with the meanings stated below:[17]

must	=	is required to
must not	=	is required not to; is disallowed
may	=	has discretion to; is permitted to
may not	=	is not permitted to; is disallowed from
is entitled to	=	has a right to
should	=	ought to
will	=	[one of the following:]
		a. (to express a future contingency)
		b. (in an adhesion contract, to express the strong party's obligations)
		c. (in a delicate contract between equals, to express both parties' obligations)

❧ Exercise 16

Revise these passages, paying special attention to your choice of words and omitting surplus words when you can. Then look at the exercise key in the Appendix.

1. All persons who are or shall have been members of the Compensation Committee (as hereinabove defined) and/or of the

Board of Directors shall be indemnified and held harmless by the Company from any loss, cost, liability, expense, charge, or obligation that is or may be imposed upon or reasonably incurred by them in connection with or resulting from any claim, action, suit, or proceeding to which they are or may be parties or in which they are or may be involved by reason of any action taken or failure to act under the Plan within.

2. "Termination of Service" in the case of an Employee shall have the meaning hereinafter stated for the purposes of this Agreement, to wit: any cessation of the employee-employer relationship between the Employee and the Company for any reason whatsoever, including, but not by way of limitation, a termination by reason of the Employee's resignation, discharge, death, disability, or retirement.

3. In the three and one-half decades just passed, the results achieved by American business have exceeded all reasonable expectations. As a result of this success, obtaining exceedingly attractive returns on investment should have been a relatively easy task for investors. Investing in a varied cross-section of securities offered by Corporate America with a view to maximizing diversification and minimizing investment costs would have accomplished the desired result. For instance, it would have been sufficient simply to acquire an index fund at the beginning of the term and then leave that investment choice entirely undisturbed. Nevertheless the results achieved by numerous investors during that period have proven to range from barely acceptable to far below the optimum.

Notes

1. For a similar list of all-purpose fuzz words, *see* Ken Smith, *Junk English* 36 (Blast Books 2001).

2. 433 U.S. 350 (1977).

3. *Id.* at 384.

4. Aristotle, *Rhetoric* 1404b, in 11 *The Works of Aristotle* (W. Ross ed. 1946).

5. "Term of art" is defined in chapter 2, above. Translated, *res ipsa loquitur* means "the thing speaks for itself." Professor Mellinkoff notes that in tort law, almost everyone understands the phrase to mean: "Ordinarily, this sort of thing wouldn't have happened unless the defendant was negligent." David Mellinkoff, *Mellinkoff's Dictionary of American Legal Usage* 560–61 (West 1992).

6. *See Restatement (Third) of Torts* §17 (Tent. Draft No. 1 2001).

7. *See, e.g.,* cases described in *Showalter v. Western Pac. R.R.,* 16 Cal. 2d 460, 106 P.2d 895 (1940).

8. 6 John Wigmore, *Evidence* §1767 at 255 (Chadbourne rev. ed. Little, Brown 1976).

9. Cal. Penal Code §597(b) (West 1999).

10. By using a definition, you avoid the need to repeat the shotgun blast time and again. The definition can be either closed-end or open-end. Each has its advantages and disadvantages. *See* Reed Dickerson, *The Fundamentals of Legal Drafting* 137–52 (2d ed. Little, Brown 1986).

In the animal abuse example, a closed-end definition would state: "abuse means ..." followed by a list of all the kinds of conduct the statute is intended to cover. One advantage of a closed-end definition is that it eliminates vagueness. One disadvantage is that the statute will not catch a villain who abuses animals in a manner not listed in the definition. The villain's lawyer will trot out the old Latin phrase *inclusio unius est exclusio alterius* and will argue that the inclusion of some types of abuse was intended to exclude other types of abuse not mentioned.

An open-end definition would state: "abuse includes but is not limited to ..." followed by a list of examples of the kinds of conduct that the statute is intended to cover. One disadvantage of an open-end definition is that it does not fully cure the vagueness problem. *See* David Mellinkoff, *Legal Writing: Sense & Nonsense* 25–26 (West 1982). One advantage, however, is that the statute will probably catch the villain whose conduct offends the spirit, though not the letter, of the law.

11. *See, e.g., Texas Legislative Council Drafting Manual* §7.34 (2004); *Hawaii Legislative Drafting Manual* 21 (9th ed. 1996); *Maine Legislative Drafting Manual* pt. III, ch. 1, §10 <http://janus.state.me.us/ros/manual> (accessed May 13, 2005).

12. *See, e.g.,* G.C. Thornton, *Legislative Drafting* 103–05 (4th ed. Butterworths 1996); *Arizona Legislative Bill Drafting Manual* 81 (2003).

13. *See* Bryan A. Garner, *A Dictionary of Modern Legal Usage* 939–42 (2nd ed. Oxford 1995); *see also* Bryan A. Garner, *Guidelines for Drafting and Editing Court Rules,* 169 F.R.D. 176, 212 (1997); G.C. Thornton, *Legislative Drafting* 103–05.

14. Joseph Kimble, *The Many Misuses of "Shall,"* 3 Scribes J. Legal Writing 61 (1992); Kenneth A. Adams, *A Manual of Style for Contract Drafting* 22–40 (ABA

2004); Kenneth A. Adams, *Legal Usage in Drafting Corporate Agreements* 22–39 (Quorum 2001); Bryan A. Garner, *A Dictionary of Modern Legal Usage* 940–41.

15. *See, e.g.*, *Arizona Legislative Bill Drafting Manual* 86 (2003); *Bill Drafting Manual for the Kentucky General Assembly* §303 (2004); *Texas Legislative Council Drafting Manual* §7.30 (2004).

16. The British Commonwealth view is expressed in New Zealand Law Commission, *Legislation Manual—Structure and Style* 43 (1996); G.C. Thornton, *Legislative Drafting* at 103–04; Robert Eagleson & Michele Asprey, *Must We Continue with "Shall"?* 63 Austl. L. J. 75 (1989), and their sequel, *id.* at 726 (1989); Martin Cutts, *The Plain English Guide* 36–37 (Oxford 1995). U.S. authors who agree include Joseph Kimble, *The Many Misuses of "Shall,"* 3 Scribes J. Legal Writing 61 (1992); David Mellinkoff, *Mellinkoff's Dictionary of American Legal Usage* at 402–03 ("unless context can be made crystal clear, prefer *must* or *required* to *shall*"); Bryan A. Garner, *A Dictionary of Modern Legal Usage* at 939–42. For purposes of contract drafting, Kenneth Adams advocates a more precise approach. He recommends using *shall* for one purpose only: to impose a duty on the subject of the sentence. He recommends using *must* to impose a duty on someone other than the subject of the sentence, or better still, changing the sentence around to impose the duty on the subject of the sentence, using *shall*. Kenneth A. Adams, *A Manual of Style for Contract Drafting* 22–30.

17. The chart is a slightly changed version of one contained in Bryan A. Garner, *A Dictionary of Modern Legal Usage* at 942.

Chapter 8

Avoid Language Quirks

Language quirks are small distractions that draw your reader's mind from *what* you are saying to *how* you are saying it. Most of what lawyers write is read by people, not because they want to, but because they have to. Their attention is therefore prone to wander. Further, they are usually surrounded by outside distractions—the ring of the telephone, the cough at the library table, and the clock that tells them time is short. Language quirks add to those distractions and thus should be avoided.

To take a simple example, most people have been told by some well-meaning teacher never to split an infinitive. An infinitive is split when a modifier is inserted between the word *to* and the verb, for example, "to never split." Even though this "rule" has been thoroughly debunked by experts,[1] it remains implanted in some readers' minds. Those readers will be distracted when they see an infinitive split unnecessarily. Therefore, do not split an infinitive unless doing so will avoid an ambiguity or a clumsy expression.[2] Likewise, do not end a sentence with a preposition unless you have to.

Avoid Elegant Variation

Elegant variation is practiced by writers whose English teachers told them not to use the same word twice in close proximity. Elegant variation produces sentences like this:

> The first case was settled for $200,000, and the second piece of litigation was disposed of out of court for $300,000, while the price of the amicable accord reached in the third suit was $500,000.

The readers are left to ponder the difference between a *case, a piece of litigation,* and a *suit.* By the time they conclude that there is no difference, they have no patience left for *settled, disposed of out of court,* and *amicable accord,* much less for what the writer was trying to tell them in the first place.

Elegant variation is particularly vexing in technical legal writing. The reader of a legal document is entitled to assume that a shift in terms is intended to signal a shift in meaning, and the reader is justifiably puzzled at passages like this:

> The use fee shall be 1% of Franchisee's gross revenue. Franchise payment shall be made on or before the 15th day of each month.

Are *franchise payments* something different from the *use fee?* If so, what are they, and when must the use fee be paid?

Do not be afraid to repeat a word if it is the right word and if repeating it will avoid confusion.

A different, but related, language quirk is the use of a word in one sense and its repetition shortly after in a different sense:

> The majority opinion gives no consideration to appellant's argument that no consideration was given for the promise.

The remedy is obvious—replace one of the pair with a different term:

> The majority opinion ignores appellant's argument that no consideration was given for the promise.

Avoid Noun Chains

A long chain of nouns used as adjectives is likely to strangle the reader. That is, noun chains create *noun chain reader strangulation problems.* Bureaucrats love noun chains. They write about *draft laboratory animal rights protection regulations* and about *public service research dissemination program proposals.* Indeed, my own law school once appointed an *Informal Discrimination Complaint Resolution Advisor.*

To bring a noun chain under control, lop off any of the descriptive words that are not essential. If that is not enough, then insert some words to break up the chain, like this: *"draft regulations to protect the rights of laboratory animals."*

Avoid Multiple Negatives

Beware of sentences that contain more than one negative expression. "It shall be unlawful to fail to ..." is an example of a double negative. The grammar is proper, but the construction is distracting—it makes the reader's mind flip from *yes* to *no* to *yes.*

In addition to ordinary negative words and prefixes (such as *not, un-,* and *non-*), many other words operate negatively (for example, *terminate, void, denial, except, unless,* and *other than*). If you string a few of these negative words together, you can make the reader's eyes cross, like this:

> Provided *however,* that this license shall *not* become *void unless* licensee's *failure* to provide such notice is *unreasonable* in the circumstances.

When you find that you have written a sentence with multiple negatives, identify each negative term. Then pair as many of them as you can to turn them into positives. Finally, rewrite the sentence using as many positives and as few negatives as you can.[3] For instance, "it shall be unlawful to fail to stop at a red light" becomes "you must stop at a red light."

Here is a more complicated passage:

> No rate agreement shall qualify under Section 2(a) unless not fewer than thirty days notice is given to all customers; and unless said rate agreement has been published, as provided above, provided however, that the publication requirement shall not apply to emergency rates; and until said rate agreement has been approved by the Commission.

When rewritten in the positive, the passage emerges like this:

> To qualify under Section 2(a), a rate agreement must meet these three conditions:
> - All customers must receive at least thirty days notice of it; and
> - It must be published, as provided above (but emergency rates do not have to be published); and
> - It must be approved by the Commission.

Avoid Cosmic Detachment

Every legal problem involves people. Without people, there would be no legal problems. Yet legal writing too often ignores people and addresses itself to some bloodless, timeless cosmic void. For example, here is the opening substantive sentence of the federal copyright law:

> Copyright protection subsists, in accordance with this title, in original works of authorship fixed in any tangible medium of expression, now known or later developed, from which they can be perceived, reproduced, or otherwise communicated, either directly or with the aid of a machine or device.[4]

Can you find any people in that sentence? *Authorship* is as close as you can get, and it is none too human.

When you find yourself struggling to express a complex legal idea, remember to ask yourself the key question that you learned in chapter 2: "Who is doing what to whom?" Bring those living creatures into your writing; make them move around and do things to each other. Suddenly abstraction will evaporate, and your writing will come alive.

Remember, too, that your reader is the most important person in the universe—or at least your reader thinks so. Don't be afraid to bring the readers into your sentences, and don't be afraid to call them "you." The personal form of address will help them understand how the passage relates to them.[5]

Use Strong Nouns and Verbs

Most legal writing is declaratory. It simply states the facts, without comment, and without trying to persuade anyone of anything. Statutes, apartment leases, corporate bylaws, and bills of lading fall in this category. But some legal writing does comment. Through commentary, it seeks to persuade the reader to believe what the writer believes. Legal briefs and judicial opinions are obvious examples. Where commentary is appropriate, it will be more potent if you use strong nouns and verbs, not weak nouns and verbs held afloat by adjectives and adverbs. For instance:

Adjectives and Adverbs	Nouns and Verbs
The witness intentionally testified untruthfully about the cargo.	The witness lied about the cargo.
Defendant's sales agents maliciously took advantage of people with little money and limited intelligence.	Defendant's sales agents preyed on the poor and the ignorant.

When you need to use a strong word for commentary, choose one that fits. Do not use a fiery one and then douse it with water:

rather catastrophic
somewhat terrified
a bit malevolently
slightly hysterical

Similarly, do not choose a flaccid one and then try to prop it up with words like *very* and *quite*:

Weak	Strong
she was very, very angry	she was enraged
this is quite puzzling	this is baffling

Avoid Sexist Language

The very first section of the United States Code says that "words importing the masculine gender include the feminine as well."[6] That may be so in the statute books, but many readers, both women and men, will be distracted and perhaps offended if you use masculine terms to refer to people who are not necessarily male.[7] On the other hand, many readers will be distracted by clumsy efforts to avoid masculine terms. In recent years, some legal writers have started using only feminine terms, but that too is distracting. Given the nature of the English language, avoiding sex bias gracefully is no easy task. Here are four suggestions that may help:

First, don't use expressions that imply value judgments based on sex. (For example, *a manly effort*, or *a member of the gentle sex*.)

Second, use sex-neutral terms if you can do so without artificiality. (For example, use *workers* instead of *workmen* and *reasonable person* instead of *reasonable man*. But don't concoct artificial terms like *waitpersons* to refer to servers in a restaurant.)

Third, use parallel construction when you are referring to both sexes. (For example, *husbands and wives*, not *men and their wives*, or *President and Mrs. Watson*, not *President Watson and Mildred*.)

Fourth, try to avoid using a sex-based pronoun when the referent may not be of that sex. For instance, don't use *he* every time you refer to judges. You can resort to the clumsy phrase *he or she* in moderation, but you can often avoid the need by using one of the following devices:

- Omit the pronoun. For example, instead of *"the average citizen enjoys his time on the jury,"* you can say *"the average citizen enjoys jury duty."*
- Use the second person instead of the third person. For example, instead of *"each juror must think for herself,"* you can say *"as a juror, you must think for yourself."*
- Use the plural instead of the singular. For example, instead of *"each juror believes that he has done something worthwhile,"* you can say *"all jurors believe that they have done something worthwhile."*
- Repeat the noun instead of using a pronoun. For example, instead of *"a juror's vote should reflect her own opinion,"* you can say *"a juror's vote should reflect that juror's own opinion."*
- Alternate between masculine and feminine pronouns. For example, if you use *she* to refer to judges in one paragraph, use *he* to refer to lawyers in the next paragraph. Be aware that this device may look artificial; further, if you are careless, you may perform a sex change on somebody in the middle of a paragraph.
- Use the passive voice. For the reasons explained in chapter 4, use this device only in desperation.

❧ Exercise 17

1. When you rewrite this passage, address it directly to the reader, omit surplus words, and eliminate the elegant variation:

Lawyers who practice before the courts are subject to local court rules, which govern matters of efficient court administration, such as what size paper to use for documents to be filed in court. Litigators must also be mindful of the preferences of individual judges, such as whether counsel are to stand or sit when questioning a witness. But most important to the courtroom attorney are the litigation principles that have been enshrined as rules of legal ethics. The ethics canons say, for example, that an attorney must not take a frivolous legal position, that is to say one that the attorney knows cannot be supported by the present law or by a good faith argument for changing the law. Similarly counsel must not express a personal opinion about a fact in issue or the credibility of a witness, and counsel must not make arguments to the jury that have not been supported by evidence in the record.

2. Break up the following noun chains:
    a. insurance claim management strategies
    b. post-Sarbanes-Oxley corporate governance directives
    c. programmatic terrorism prevention research proposals
    d. intramural sports injury treatment protocols
    e. symptomatic prenatal stress relief regimen

3. Revise this passage, minimizing the number of negative expressions:

This homeowner's insurance policy does not cover losses caused by the following perils, notwithstanding any other cause contributing to the loss:

✓ freezing of interior pipes that is not the result of exterior temperatures below 32 degrees F.;

✓ continuous or repeated leakage of water or steam, other than from a:
  • furnace,
  • air conditioner, or
  • fire sprinkler system
  that is not past its manufacturer's warranty period; or

✓ mechanical breakdown, except for a breakdown that is not caused directly or indirectly by the insured's negligence.

4. Revise the following passage, avoiding cosmic detachment and keeping in mind the circumstances in which it will be read:

In the unlikely event of a water landing, the area beneath your seat contains a personal flotation device. Upon being given appropriate instructions by the flight attendant, deploy the device by inserting your arms through the appropriate openings beneath the shoulders. Next, locate the nylon straps attached to the middle of the device and, using the buckle system provided, secure the straps snugly around your waist. Then, on the front of the flotation device, you will observe two red plastic tabs. Seize the two tabs with your right and left hands and tug them gently downward, which will initiate the inflation mechanism of the floatation device. *Under no circumstances* are you to inflate the device until you are given the signal to do so by the flight attendant. After inflating the device, follow all subsequent instructions given by the flight attendant.

5. Revise this passage using appropriately strong nouns and verbs rather than adjectives and adverbs:

The defendant corporation engaged in a reprehensible campaign of untruthful advertising, the object of which was to mislead people who have almost no resources and whose life experience and rudimentary schooling provide them relatively little scientific knowledge. Defendant, for the selfish purpose of augmenting its own revenues, undertook a program of misinformation, hoping to cause these unfortunate people to believe that antiretroviral drugs are causally connected with impotence, and that defendant's multi-vitamin pills are more beneficial than antiretroviral drugs in combating HIV.

6. Revise the following sentences, avoiding sexist language and surplus words when you can:

a. Not only may the judge examine witnesses called by the parties, he may also call witnesses himself whom the parties might not have called.

b. A prosecutor may sometimes inveigle the judge to call a hostile but essential witness whom the prosecutor himself needs but fears to call. When the judge calls such a witness, he can question him from the bench, which often diminishes his hostility and makes him a more useful witness.

c. Art. II, §2, says that the President herself is the Commander-in-Chief of the Army and the Navy, and it gives her the power to grant reprieves and pardons for offenses against the United States. A sitting President, then, would seemingly have the power to order one of the military officers under her command to act covertly in violation of a federal criminal statute, and then to pardon him if he were caught and prosecuted.

Notes

1. *See* Theodore Bernstein, *Miss Thistlebottom's Hobgoblins* 116–18 (1971); Henry W. Fowler, *A Dictionary of Modern English Usage* 579–82 (2nd ed. revised by Sir Ernest Gowers, Oxford 1965).

2. Henry W. Fowler, *The New Fowler's Modern English Usage* 736–38 (3rd ed. edited by R.W. Burchfield, Oxford 1996); United Press International, *UPI Style Book* 289–90 (3rd ed. 1992); Allan M. Siegal and William G. Connolly, *The New York Times Manual of Style and Usage* 312 (Times Books 1999).

3. *See* Rudolf Flesch, *How To Write Plain English: A Book for Lawyers and Consumers* 94–101 (Harper & Row 1979); *see also* David Mellinkoff, *Legal Writing: Sense & Nonsense* 28–38 (West 1982); Robert Eagleson, *Writing in Plain English* 50–51 (Australian Government Publishing Service 1990).

4. 17 U.S.C. §102 (2000).

5. *See* Robert Eagleson, *Writing in Plain English* at 49.

6. 1 U.S.C. §1 (2000).

7. *See generally*, Ronald Collins, *Language, History, and the Legal Process: A Profile of the "Reasonable Man,"* 8 Rut.-Cam. L.J. 311 (1977); Casey Miller & Kate Swift, *Words and Women* (Anchor 1977); Casey Miller and Kate Swift, *The Handbook of Nonsexist Writing* (2nd ed. iUniverse 2001); *but see* Henry W. Fowler, *The New Fowler's Modern English Usage* 705–706. Based on my experience teaching U.S. law students and legislative drafters from many other nations, I find that in the U.S. and the British Commonwealth, writers have become more careful in the past 20 years about sexist terms, and readers have become more tolerant of the occasional blunder. But elsewhere in the world, the effort to avoid sexist terms can still spark hot debate.

Chapter 9

Punctuate Carefully

How Punctuation Developed

As English speakers in the 21st century, we are accustomed to the idea that punctuation affects meaning, but our punctuation system would have seemed odd to an English speaker in the early 17th century.[1] The punctuation used in those days had evolved from earlier systems of dots, lines, and slash marks used by the Greeks and Romans.[2] The Greek and Roman systems were not syntactic; that is, punctuation marks were not intended to affect meaning and were not based on grammar, as our marks are today. Rather, the Greek and Roman marks served a rhetorical function (by dividing segments of discourse according to formal rhetorical patterns) and an elocutionary function (by indicating where to pause and breathe when reading the text aloud). Like the Greek and Roman systems, the punctuation used in early 17th century English was not syntactic; its function was primarily rhythmic and elocutionary.[3]

By the end of the 17th century, English was starting to become rule-bound. Rules of grammar, spelling, and capitalization developed.[4] About that time, our present syntactic system of punctuation was born. Our syntactic system uses punctuation marks as guides to the grammatical construction and thus to the meaning of a passage. Syntactic punctuation does not ignore rhythm and elocution. Shifts in syntax tend to coincide with pauses for emphasis or for breath in oral delivery, and modern punctuation therefore tends to reflect the patterns and rhythms of speech.

Lawyers' Distrust of Punctuation

English-speaking lawyers have traditionally distrusted punctuation as a guide to meaning. Even today in Great Britain, some solicitors prefer to draft legal instruments with almost no punctuation; they argue that punctuation is unreliable because it can capriciously disappear (as when a legal secretary has a momentary lapse of concentration) or capriciously appear (as when a fly explores the page and deposits something that could pass for a comma).[5]

Lawyers' distrust of punctuation as a guide to meaning has three sources. The first was the unreliability of punctuation in the late 17th century, and well into the 18th century, when the syntactic system was in its adolescence. Syntactic punctuation did not spring forth full-grown, nor did every writer adopt it overnight.[6] During this formative period, some writers punctuated for rhythmic and elocutionary effect, some punctuated syntactically, and some did a little of both. Thus, at that time, punctuation was indeed an unreliable guide to meaning.

The second source of distrust was the printing press, which was introduced in England in 1476. Before the printing press, statutes and other important documents were handwritten by professional scribes, and scribes trained by different masters had diverse customs for capitalization, spelling, and punctuation.[7] By the middle of the 17th century, printing had become commonplace, and the printers had a penchant for uniformity. They were known to delete or supply punctuation to make their product uniform.[8] Because the printer may have fiddled with the punctuation, it was an unreliable guide to the author's intended meaning.[9]

The third source of distrust was the old tale that English statutes were traditionally unpunctuated. Professor Mellinkoff long ago exposed that tale as a falsehood. He examined the best available sources of old handwritten statutes and concluded that "English statutes have been punctuated from the earliest days."[10] The punctuation is not like ours, and it is often sparse and inconsistent, but it is there. Nonetheless, the old tale lives on and is occasionally still cited in support of a supposed rule that judges can ignore punctuation when they interpret statutes.

Judicial decisions on both sides of the Atlantic yield a rich assortment of conflicting slogans about using punctuation as a guide to meaning. Some say that it should be ignored; others say that it can be used, but only in a pinch. Still others say that it should be considered along with all other available clues to the author's intended meaning.[11] For example, in *United States v. Ron Pair Enterprises*,[12] the United States Supreme Court split 5–4 over the significance of a comma in a bankruptcy statute. One lower federal court had called it a "capricious" comma,[13] and another had called it an awfully "small hook on which to hang a [substantial] change in the law."[14] The majority of five Supreme Court Justices, with no apology, relied partly on the comma to conclude that the statute was clear on its face. The four dissenting Justices, on the other hand, tried to obliterate the comma with a blast of slogans from old cases: punctuation is minor and not controlling, punctuation is not decisive, punctuation is the most fallible standard by which to interpret a writing, and punctuation can be changed or ignored to effectuate congressional intent.

Punctuate Carefully

The lesson that emerges is this: modern readers, including judges, do use punctuation as a guide to meaning. Trying to draft without punctuation is no good because, "if you don't punctuate, a reader will do it for you, in places you never wanted it."[15] Further, leaving the task of punctuation to a legal secretary, as some lawyers are inclined to do, is an abdication of the professional duty to express meaning as clearly as possible.

Thus, when you write, you should punctuate carefully, in accordance with ordinary English usage. The following punctuation guide conforms to ordinary English usage, as expressed in standard modern sources. These sources do not always agree with each other, and where they disagree, I have suggested the approach that will produce clarity with as little complexity as possible. This punctuation guide will not answer *all* of your punctuation questions. For that, your law office library should include some reliable, modern texts that cover grammar, style, and punctuation.[16]

Definition of Terms

Punctuation is easier if you remember a few definitions:

Subject: The word or group of words that a clause or sentence makes a statement about.

- The *lawyer* had objected to the evidence.

Predicate: The word or group of words that makes a statement about the subject. The complete predicate is the main verb plus any modifiers and complements attached to it.

- The lawyer *had objected to the evidence.*

The simple predicate is the main verb (with its helping verbs).

- The lawyer *had objected* to the evidence.

Phrase: A group of closely related words that does not contain both a subject and a predicate.

- *The lawyer in the gray skirt ...*
- *Objecting to the evidence ...*

Independent clause: A group of words that contains both a subject and a predicate and that grammatically could stand alone as a complete sentence.

- *The lawyer in the gray skirt objected to the evidence.*

Dependent clause: A group of words that contains both a subject and a predicate, but that grammatically could not stand alone as a complete sentence.

- *When the lawyer in the gray skirt objected to the evidence ...*

A dependent clause frequently begins with a subordinating word, such as *who, which, when, that, since,* or *because.*

A dependent clause can function as an adjective, an adverb, or a noun.

- The lawyer *who wore the gray skirt* objected to the evidence. [adjective—describes lawyer]
- *When she objected,* the judge sustained the objection. [adverb—tells when]
- The judge agreed *that the evidence was inadmissible.* [noun—tells what]

Commas

We begin with commas, because commas (or the lack of them) cause more mischief in the law than all of the other punctuation marks combined.

Use a comma when you link independent clauses with a coordinating conjunction

An independent clause can stand on its own as a complete sentence. When you use a coordinating conjunction (*and, but, or, for, nor, yet,* and *so*) to link two independent clauses into one sentence, you must put a comma before the conjunction. In 25 years of teaching advanced legal writing to third-year law students, I have found this to be the most common punctuation error.

- The defendant intentionally accessed the government computer system, and he intentionally denied access to authorized users.

- The "worm" that the defendant inserted in the computer system multiplied a million-fold, yet the defendant claimed that he did not intend to damage the system.

To join two independent clauses properly, you need both the comma and the conjunction. (If you use only the comma without the conjunction, you will be guilty of a "comma splice," a grievous sin.) Another way to join two independent clauses properly is with a semicolon; when you do that, you ordinarily do not use a conjunction.

- The defendant's computer sabotage cost the government at least ten thousand hours of lost computer time; it also destroyed valuable, irreplaceable data.

Use a comma after introductory elements

Put a comma after an introductory phrase or clause.

- Wanting to settle the case quickly, the plaintiff authorized her lawyer to accept any amount over $5,000.

- At the time of the accident, the defendant was intoxicated.

- To make the point clearly, she used a diagram.

If the introductory element is very short, omit the comma.

- At home he wears glasses instead of contact lenses.

Omit the comma if the introductory element is followed by inverted word order.

- From the apartment above came a loud scream.

Use commas to set off nonrestrictive elements

A nonrestrictive element within a sentence modifies or describes part of the sentence but is not essential to the meaning of the sentence. Set off nonrestrictive elements with commas. Elements beginning with *which, although,* or *though* are usually nonrestrictive.

- The car, which is blue, ran the red light.

In contrast, a restrictive element is essential to the meaning of the sentence, and it should not be set off with commas. Elements beginning with *that, because, before, while, if,* or *when* are usually restrictive.

- The car that ran the red light was blue.

To determine whether an element is restrictive or nonrestrictive, try mentally eliminating it from the sentence. If the meaning changes, or the sentence becomes ambiguous, the information is restrictive and should *not* be set off with commas.

- His father, who is an engineer, arrived on Tuesday.
- The corporation, which has its principal place of business in Alaska, is engaged in oil and gas exploration.
- The job that she was seeking was filled.

When a dependent clause comes at the beginning of a sentence, always put a comma at the end of it, even if it is restrictive.

- If you accept our conditions, we will postpone the hearing.

Use commas to set off parenthetical elements

When you insert a parenthetical element into a sentence, put a comma on both ends of it. A parenthetical element is one that is pertinent but not essential to the meaning of the sentence. If a word, phrase, or clause could be deleted without affecting the meaning of the sentence, then set it off with commas.

- The mayor's indictment was, to say the least, unexpected.
- Freedom of speech is, after all, one of our most cherished rights.

Legal citations included in the text are parentheticals and should be set off by commas.

- In the *DeShaney* case, 489 U.S. at 192, that very point was discussed by the Court.

Use commas to separate the items in a series

When a sentence contains a series of three or more items joined with one conjunction, put commas after each item except the last.

- The defendant was armed with a sawed-off shotgun, a semi-automatic pistol, and a hunting knife when he entered the bank.

If the series is complicated or contains internal commas, use semicolons rather than commas between the items.

- The police search of the suspect's apartment produced engraving plates, which were of the type used for counterfeiting; a large quantity of ink, which apparently had been stolen from the government's ink supplier; and a variety of forged passports and other travel documents, which showed that the suspect had recently traveled to nine European countries.

Use commas to separate coordinate adjectives

When two or more adjectives are "coordinate," they modify a noun equally, and they should be separated with commas. Do not put a comma between the last adjective and the noun.

- The plaintiff was driving an old, rattly, blue truck.

If the last adjective and the noun together form the term that is modified by the prior adjectives, do not use a comma before the last adjective.

- The plaintiff was driving an old, rattly Ford truck.

If one adjective modifies another, do not separate them with a comma. To tell whether the adjectives are equal modifiers (and thus should be separated with commas), try mentally rearranging the adjectives or mentally inserting the word *and* between the adjectives. If the meaning does not change, the adjectives are equal modifiers (coordinates), and you should use a comma to separate them.

- A dark, cold night (*dark* and *cold* modify *night* equally).

- A bright red tie (*bright* modifies *red*; a "red, bright tie" states a different meaning).

- A strong constitutional argument (*constitutional argument* is the term modified by *strong*).

Use commas to set off transitional or interrupting words and phrases

Use commas to set off transitional words (*therefore, thus, furthermore, moreover,* and the like) at the beginning or in the middle of a sentence.

- The conclusion, therefore, is that attorney advertising deserves only limited protection under the First Amendment.

If the transitional word is between two independent clauses, put a semicolon in front of it and a comma after it.

- Attorney advertising is a type of commercial speech; therefore, it deserves only limited protection under the First Amendment.

If a term of direct address (*madam, sir, my friend,* and the like) interrupts a sentence, set it off with commas.

- We submit, Your Honor, that the injunction should be lifted.

Use commas to set off dates, titles, geographic names, and short quotations

Respected modern sources differ about the use of commas in writing dates. These are the commonly recommended formats:

- On December 21, 2012, the winter solstice sun will be centered in the "dark rift" of the Milky Way.
- On 21 December 2012, the winter solstice sun will be centered in the "dark rift" of the Milky Way.
- The Mayan calendar ends on December 21st of 2012.

Titles that follow a person's name are usually nonrestrictive and should be set off with commas.

- Jane Sherwood, M.D., testified for the defense.
- Jake Michaels, Esq., is the youngest partner.

Use commas to separate geographic place names (cities from states, and states from nations).

- Seattle, Washington, is the defendant's principal place of business.
- Tokyo, Japan, is the plaintiff's principal place of business.

Use a comma to introduce a short quotation, unless it is incorporated into your sentence.

- The witness said, "The red car was speeding."
- The statute banned smoking "in any public building."

Semicolons

Some writers put semicolons and wild mushrooms in the same category: some are delicious, but others are deadly, and since it is hard to tell the difference, they should all be avoided. In truth, semicolons are not hard to master, and they can be very useful.

Use a semicolon to join two independent clauses without a conjunction

You can use a semicolon without a conjunction to join two closely related independent clauses; doing so adds variety to your writing and helps keep it from seeming choppy. Do not, however, join two independent clauses with a semicolon unless they are closely related, as these are:

- The defense counsel objected to the question; she said that it called for information protected by the attorney-client privilege.

- Plaintiff Munoz had just witnessed his wife's death; he was in a state of deep shock.

Use a semicolon when two independent clauses are joined by a transitional expression

When you use a transitional expression (such as *therefore, however, furthermore, thus, indeed, in fact, as a result,* or *for example*) to join two independent clauses, put a semicolon before the transitional word or phrase, and put a comma after it.

- The court granted the preliminary injunction; therefore, the company could not fire the plaintiff while the case was pending.

- The witness had no personal knowledge of the event; in truth, her testimony was hearsay.

- Her testimony could have been admitted under several exceptions to the hearsay rule; for example, either the excited utterance exception or the contemporaneous statements exception would apply.

Use semicolons to separate the items in a complicated series

Ordinarily you should use commas to separate the items in a series, as explained above. But, if the series is complicated or contains internal commas, use semicolons to separate the items.

- The prosecutor called the following witnesses: Susan Wu, a psychiatrist; Michael Bradford, a ballistics expert; and George Frye, a police investigator.

Colons

A colon indicates that what follows is a summary or elaboration of what precedes it, or is a series, or is a long quotation.

Use a colon to introduce a series

When you use a colon to introduce a series, the material that precedes the colon must be able to stand alone as an independent clause.

The independent clause can include *as follows* or *the following*, but it need not do so.

- We must subpoena the following witnesses: Barnes, Cruz, and Younger.

- We must subpoena three witnesses: Barnes, Cruz, and Younger.

Do not put a colon between a verb and its object or between a preposition and its object.

- We must subpoena: Barnes, Cruz, and Younger. (The colon is misused here because it separates the verb *subpoena* from its three objects.)

- We must serve a subpoena on: Barnes, Cruz, and Younger. (The colon is misused here because it separates the preposition *on* from its three objects.)

Use a colon to introduce a summary, elaboration, or illustration

- The plaintiff failed to prove two key elements: negligence and proximate cause.

- The damages were staggering: $1,948,000 in medical bills and $74,000 in lost wages.

- Only one thing stands between us and settlement: money.

You can also use a colon to join two independent clauses if the first clause introduces the second, or if the two clauses have a cause and effect relationship.

- The DNA evidence is vital: it is our only proof that the defendant was at the scene.

- The gasoline truck hit the wall: the gasoline explosion killed the driver.

Use a colon to introduce a long quotation

You should ordinarily use a comma to introduce a short quotation, but if the quotation is longer than one sentence, then use a colon.

- She invoked the words of Abraham Lincoln: "The Lord prefers common-looking people. That is the reason He makes so many of them."

Dashes

Use dashes to signal an abrupt break

Commas, parentheses, and dashes are all used to set off material that interrupts a sentence. The three differ in the emphasis they give to the material they set off. Commas tend to be neutral; they neither emphasize nor play down the material. Parentheses tend to play down the material, to make it clearly subordinate. Dashes tend to emphasize the material.

- The judge—bristling with indignation—slammed his gavel on the bench.

- We need not reach the constitutional issue—that can await another day and another set of facts.

Use dashes, not commas, when you need to clearly set off a lump of material that needs to sit in the middle of a sentence because of what it modifies.[17]

- The magistrate may rule on any procedural motion—including a motion to suppress evidence and a motion to allow or disallow discovery—at any time following the acceptance of a plea.

Parentheses

Use parentheses to set off interjected or explanatory material

Like commas and dashes, parentheses can be used to set off material that interrupts a sentence. Parentheses tend to play down the material that is set off, to make it clearly subordinate.

- The police found a diamond ring (worth at least $1,000) in the suspect's pants pocket.

The material inside the parentheses should be punctuated as necessary.

- In the suspect's pants pocket, the police found a diamond ring (worth at least $1,000) and three credit cards (a MasterCard, a Visa card, and an American Express card).

Use parentheses to avoid ambiguities

Used in moderation, parentheses (and their big brothers, brackets) can be helpful when you need to clarify what modifies what, or to interject a brief definition or qualification, or to state an exception.

- [The levy established in subparagraph 9 does not, however, apply to residential property (property used by a taxpayer as a primary residence).]

- No deduction is allowed if the donor retains or transfers an interest (as defined above) in the property to any person other than the donee spouse (or the estate of the spouse).

Use parentheses when you want to label the items in a series

When a sentence lists several complex elements in a series, you can use numbers or letters enclosed in parentheses to indicate the intended divisions.

- The testator gave her sister-in-law three items: (a) 100 shares of Intel common stock, (b) the amethyst ring that had belonged to the testator's Aunt Dolores, and (c) an ancient calico cat, which had been the testator's constant companion.

Use parentheses to introduce shorthand expressions you will use later

- The Eastern Region Trade Agreement (ERTA) prohibits any retaliatory tariff on agricultural commodities.
- Universal Communications, Inc. (UCI) developed the transverse uniflex modulator system ("the system") in 1994.

Apostrophes

Use apostrophes to form possessives

Modern authorities differ on how to form some possessives. Be aware that reasonable people can disagree passionately about the following rules (one wonders whether there are not grander things to worry about). To make the possessive of a singular noun, add 's, even if the word ends with an *s* sound. If that would make a triple *s* sound, then use an apostrophe only. For classical and biblical names that end in *s*, use an apostrophe only.

- Susan's opera cape
- Theodore James's new novel
- Defendant Jones's fingerprints
- Achilles' heel

- Zacharias' son, John the Baptist

To make the possessive of a plural noun that ends in an *s* sound, use an apostrophe only. If the plural ends in a different sound, use *'s*.

- The women's restroom
- The Joneses' house
- The clans' movement across the desert

If more than one owner is listed, you must decide whether the ownership is joint or individual. For joint ownership, form the possessive for the last owner listed. For individual ownership, form the possessive for each owner listed.

- Jesse's and Ula Mae's computers (each owns one)
- Bruce and Tim's sailboat (they own it together)

For compound expressions, form the possessive with the last element listed.

- The plaintiff was driving her mother-in-law's car.
- Your Honors' original order required payment of costs. (several judges entered the order)

Never put an apostrophe in a possessive pronoun (his, hers, its, yours, ours, theirs, whose). Remember that *its* is the possessive pronoun meaning "belonging to it." *It's* is the contraction for "it is." Finally, if your ear tells you that a possessive sounds awkward, be bold and use a few glue words to form the possessive the long way. For example, "the index of the revised and expanded edition" is longer but sounds better than "the revised and expanded edition's index."

Use *'s* to form the plural of some terms

Use *'s* to form the plural of abbreviations, numbers, letters, symbols, and words referred to as words. The modern trend is not to use an apostrophe in the plurals of years.

- Revise this contract by replacing all the aforementioned's with this's.
- The witness recalled that the license number included three 6's.

- She got mostly B's in law school.
- C.P.A.'s usually enjoy the tax courses.
- The Impressionists dominated the late 1800s.

Use apostrophes in contractions and abbreviations

In contractions and abbreviations, an apostrophe stands for the omitted letters. For example, *can't, it's, wouldn't, Nat'l,* and *Ass'n.* Because contractions convey informality, you should not use them in drafting statutes, court orders, contracts, appellate briefs, or other formal legal documents. They are, however, appropriate if you want a piece of legal writing to have an informal tone. For example, some judges favor contractions in jury instructions because the informal tone is consistent with their personal style in delivering the instructions orally to the jury. They are also appropriate if you want to set an informal tone in a client letter, an office memorandum, or even in a chatty law review article.

Hyphens

Check compound terms in an up-to-date dictionary

Some compound terms (terms that are formed from more than one word) are written as separate words (*ice cream*), some are hyphenated (*brother-in-law*), and some are written as a single word (*textbook*). Usage often changes over time. A compound term usually enters the language as two words (*hard disk*). As it becomes more familiar, it often grows a hyphen (*freeze-dried*). When it becomes commonplace, it often becomes one word (*handlebar*). When you are in doubt, check the term in an up-to-date dictionary.

Follow common usage in hyphenating compound modifiers

If two or more words act together as a single modifier, they should usually be joined by hyphens. Some of these compound modifiers are common and can be found in a dictionary (*second-guess*), but others are created to fit the need (*nursing-home care*). The following general principles, plus a large measure of your own common sense, will help avoid hyphen errors like this one: "The new tax deduction is designed to aid small business owners." (Apparently the large ones must fend for themselves.)

Hyphenate only when the modifier precedes the term modified.

- My hard-headed boss
- My boss is hard headed.

Do not hyphenate if the first term is an adverb ending in *-ly*.

- An overly active imagination
- A radically different constitutional analysis

Do not hyphenate foreign phrases.

- A bona fide purchaser
- An ex post facto law

A hyphen is usually used with the prefixes *ex-, self-, quasi-,* and *all-*. A hyphen is usually not used after the prefixes *anti, co, de, inter, intra, multi, non, para, pro, re, semi,* or *super*—unless the second element is capitalized or the hyphen is needed to avoid confusion.

- Her ex-husband
- A self-inflicted wound
- The quasi-contract claim
- Antitrust law
- The anti-Communist forces
- Her paralegal assistant
- His redrafted brief

If two or more hyphenated compounds share a common element, the shared element can be used only once.

- Long- and short-term budget reductions
- Pre- and post-judgment interest

Use hyphens for compound numbers and fractions

Use hyphens for numbers twenty-one through ninety-nine, even if they are part of a larger number.

- Thirty-eight
- One hundred thirty-eight

Use hyphens between all elements of a fraction.

- A one-third contingent fee
- A one-twenty-sixth share

Use a hyphen to divide a word at the end of a line

When you must break a word at the end of a line, use a hyphen, and make the break between syllables. Check your dictionary for the syllable divisions. Word processing programs that insert hyphens automatically are not infallible, so stay alert. Do not divide a word over a page break or leave a one-letter syllable standing lonely on the end of a line. By the way, you can avoid the whole issue by using a ragged (unjustified) right-hand margin, which also makes reading easier for some people and which avoids distracting oddities in the spacing between words.

Periods, Question Marks, and Exclamation Points

Use a period to end a declarative sentence, a command, or an indirect quotation

- Serve the interrogatories today.
- She asked what day the interrogatory answers are due.

Follow common usage in putting periods in abbreviations

Some abbreviations use periods, and others do not. You can look up common abbreviations in a good dictionary, or the ALWD Citation Manual, or the Bluebook.[18] If you cannot find the abbreviation in those sources, you probably should not use it, unless your readers are sure to know what you are talking about. If an abbreviation with a period at the end comes at the close of a sentence, use only one period.

Use a question mark to end direct questions

Put a question mark at the end of a direct question.

- To what extent is hate speech protected by the First Amendment?
- What would justify a writ of mandamus in this case?

Do not put a question mark at the end of a request or command that is courteously phrased as a question.

- Will you please have the memorandum to me by tomorrow.
- Would counsel kindly take his feet off the conference table.

Do not put a question mark at the end of an indirect question.

- The judge asked why our brief exceeded the page limit.
- Why, she said, did we file such a long brief.

Use exclamation points rarely

Exclamation points, which show surprise or strong emotion, are much like chili peppers. Used sparingly and in the right context, they add a piquant touch, but be careful. In formal legal writing, such as an appellate brief, exclamation points are almost never appropriate: they tend to be strident rather than persuasive. But, in a client letter or office memorandum, the occasional exclamation point will do no harm; if nothing else, it lets the writer blow off steam.

Quotations

Enclose short, direct quotations in quotation marks

Use double (") quotation marks to surround direct quotations of under fifty words. Alternate between double and single (') marks for material quoted within a quotation. For quotations of fifty words or more, indent on both the left and right, and leave any internal quote marks the way you found them in the original. Put commas and periods inside quotation marks; other punctuation marks belong outside unless they are part of the quoted material.

Indicate deletions, alterations, and additions to quoted material

Use square brackets around anything you add to or change in a quotation, such as when you add an explanatory word, or change a plural to a singular, or change a letter from upper to lower case, or vise versa. An ellipsis (...) is three periods separated by spaces and with a space at each end. Generally, use an ellipsis to indicate an omission. Do not, however, use an ellipsis to begin a quotation, and do not use ellipses when you are quoting only a phrase or clause, rather than a full sentence.[19]

❧ Exercise 18

In the following sentences, correct the punctuation and spelling. When necessary, change the wording to make properly constructed sentences. Some of the sentences are correct as written. When you finish, look at the exercise key in the Appendix.

1. From 1776 until the end of the War of 1812 the overriding question was whether the nation, besieged without by hos-

tile governments and within by provincialism, having sufficient power to survive.

2. During those formative years, the weakest of the three branches of government being the judiciary.

3. Not particularly brightening the outlook, President Adam's appointment of John Marshall to the Court in 1801, supported unenthusiastically even by the Federalist's.

4. Yet, in its first 10 years under John Marshalls' guidance the Court consolidated far reaching judicial power and in another 15 it put Congress' authority on a broad and permanent constitutional footing.

5. The Jeffersonians' were certain of two things; that the Constitution was a limiting document and John Marshall was a malignant force.

6. They charged the Chief Justice with usurping power, and with converting his weak willed colleagues to his plans for aggrandizement.

7. The Federalists', on the other-hand expected the Court to consolidate national power, and contain the emerging forces of democracy.

8. There is precedent for non judicial action, by allies against a former enemy leader whose acts seem abhorrent, that of Napoleon.

9. When Napoleon escaped from Elba, broke the 1814 peace treaty and marched again on Europe he was declared "*hors la loi*" that is "beyond the law" by representatives of all the European states, except France which left the question what to do about him.

10. The Prussians said shoot him and the Russians said more delicately "summary execution."

11. Ultimately, however the Europeans agreed to exile him, to St. Helena where he would be out of the way and kept at British expense.

12. Exile spared the embarrassment of executing a sovereign, all European rulers had condemned the execution of Louis XVI, and did not want their subjects to suppose that killing rulers was an acceptable way of expressing their opinion of them.

13. No-one seriously considered a trial for Napoleon, it was unnecessary since his crimes were self-evident condemnation was universal and the European leaders had no qualms about punishing him for them.

14. However the idea of a trial for Nazi war-criminals was attractive to many even though the form the proponents favored was repugnant to others.

15. Stalin had punished his opponents and frightened others by "show trials" in the 1930's and Hitler himself mounted a show-trial for those who plotted to take his life in July, 1944.

16. In a show trial one can even allow a little defense; just enough to demonstrate how feeble it is.

17. The US Supreme Court has held that the processing, and disposal of solid-waste in landfills concerns an article-of-commerce for purposes of Commerce Clause analysis.

18. The legal issue in this case is whether the article-of-commerce test is satisfied when applied to sewage sludge the substance in question here.

19. Sewage-sludge is a by product of wastewater treatment. It is generally a solid or semi solid mud like substance, typically consisting of water and from 2–28% solids.

20. Some people limit the term 'sewage sludge' to mean stabilized disinfected sewage sludge that is suitable for beneficial agricultural uses.

21. Sewage sludge differs from solid-waste; in that economic ecological and agricultural benefits are realized by farmers using treated-sewage-sludge as fertilizer.

22. If solid waste constitutes an article-of-commerce, an even stronger more persuasive case can be made for regarding sewage sludge as an article of commerce for Commerce-Clause purposes.

23. Plaintiff Lutz sued defendant Reliance Nissan for wrongful termination and defendant successfully moved to compel arbitration pursuant to a two tiered arbitration procedure, that was specified by her employment contract.

24. Lutz won the initial arbitration but upon a second tier review the 'appellate' arbitrator reversed Lutz' award, and entered an award for defendant which award was confirmed by the trial court.

25. In a pre-mature appeal from the trial courts confirmation order Lutz raises various meritless arguments.

26. We hold that Lutz is responsible for the delay of which she complains, that she suffered no harm because defendant paid for all arbitration costs, that the two tiered procedure, which is uncommon but not unconscionable, was contractually binding, and, most important that the contract permissibly invested the "appellate' arbitrator with a broader standard of review than an appellate court would ordinarily have.

27. Our economic system depends in part on: legal recognition of property rights, and the ability of parties to enforce contract rights when necessary.

28. Defendant is charged with three antitrust offenses: horizontal price-fixing, horizontal division of territories, and resale price maintenance.

29. Patents protect novel and nonobvious inventions, such as machines, medicines, and processes; in contrast, copyrights protect original works of authorship, such as books, music, and paintings.

30. Attorney conflicts of interest can arise with: present clients, prospective clients, and former clients.

31. The most common causes of attorney discipline are: alcohol and greed.

32. Defense counsel sat in silence; the prosecutor's evidence was admitted.

33. This is the way a pleading ends: not with a Bang but a Wherefore.

34. Our deadlines shorter now, because of the one-year statute of limitations.

35. The peoples' right to be secure in their persons, houses, papers, and effects, against unreasonable search's and seizure's shall not be violated.

36. Its important to listen to our instincts when assessing a legal arguments' validity.

37. Lay witnesses can be paid for their expenses and time lost from work, but a lay witness's request for additional payments cannot be granted.

38. Justice O'Connors' concurring opinion took issue with the majoritys reliance on cases from the 1920s, before the expansion of Congress' power under the Commerce Clause. Her's is the more persuasive of the two opinion's.

39. A business' net worth is not always a good measure of it's future profitability.

40. Microsofts Bill Gates's public image improved when his' contributions to various charitable and educational causes' increased.

41. "Who's brown satchel is that beside the witnesses stand, and whats it doing there?" the judge asked in a quiet voice.

Notes

1. Parts of this chapter are drawn from Richard Wydick, *Should Lawyers Punctuate?*, 1 Scribes J. of Leg. Writing 7 (1990). The history of punctuation in legal writing is related in David Mellinkoff, *The Language of the Law* 152–70 (Little, Brown 1963).

2. *See* Joseph Robertson, *An Essay on Punctuation* 1–14 (1785), reproduced in facsimile, *English Linguistics 1500–1800*, No. 168 (Scolar Press 1969); Robert Peters, *A Linguistic History of English* 298–99 (Houghton, Mifflin 1968).

3. *See* Simon Daines, *Orthoepia Anglicana* 70–73 (1640), reproduced in facsimile, *English Linguistics 1500–1800*, No. 31 (Scolar Press 1967); *see also* Mindele Treip, *Milton's Punctuation and Changing English Usage 1582–1676*, 27–28 (Methuen Pub. 1970).

4. *See* Albert Baugh & Thomas Cable, *A History of the English Language* 253–94 (3rd ed. Prentice-Hall 1978); Barbara Strang, *A History of English* 104–55 (Methuen Pub. 1970).

5. *See* Wydick, *Should Lawyers Punctuate?* 7–10. Reed Dickerson, a respected U.S. authority on legal drafting, similarly distrusted punctuation. He said the careful legal drafter should use punctuation as a "finishing device," but "should not rely solely on it to do what an arrangement of words can do." Reed Dickerson, *The Fundamentals of Legal Drafting* 188 (2nd ed. Little, Brown 1986).

6. *See* Treip, *Milton's Punctuation and Changing English Usage* 16–17, 35–53.

7. *See* Strang, *A History of English* 107–10, 157–59.

8. *See, e.g.*, Percy Simpson, *Shakesperian Punctuation* 7–15 (Clarendon 1911); Treip, *Milton's Punctuation and Changing English Usage* 14–34.

9. *See* Mellinkoff, *The Language of the Law* 163.

10. *Id.* at 157–64.

11. *See* authorities collected in Wydick, *Should Lawyers Punctuate?* 19–22.

12. 489 U.S. 235 (1989). *See also, Smith v. City of Jackson, Mississippi,* ___ U.S. ___, ___, 126 S. Ct. 1536, 1550 (2005) (O'Connor, Kennedy, and Thomas, JJ., concurring).

13. *In re Dan-Ver Enter.,* 67 Bankr. 951 (W.D. Pa. 1986).

14. *In re Newbury Cafe,* 841 F.2d 20, 22 (1st Cir. 1988), *vacated and remanded sub nom., Massachusetts v. Gray,* 489 U.S. 1049 (1989).

15. David Mellinkoff, *Legal Writing: Sense & Nonsense* 57 (West 1982).

16. The choices are legion and include the following: Bryan A. Garner, *The Redbook: A Manual on Legal Style* (West 2002); *The Chicago Manual of Style* (15th ed. Chicago 2003); Allan M. Siegal & William G. Connolly, *The New York Times Manual of Style and Usage* (Times Books 2003); Frederick Crews, *The Random House Handbook* (6th ed. McGraw-Hall 1991); Lynn Quitman Troyka & Douglas Hesse, *Simon & Schuster Handbook for Writers* (7th ed. Prentice Hall 2004).

17. Bryan A. Garner, *Guidelines for Drafting and Editing Court Rules,* 169 F.R.D. 176, 195 (1997).

18. Darby Dickerson, *Association of Legal Writing Directors Citation Manual* (Aspen 2000); *The Bluebook: A Uniform System of Citation* (18th ed. Harv. L. Rev. Ass'n 2005), compiled by the editors of the Columbia Law Review, the Harvard Law Review, the University of Pennsylvania Law Review, and the Yale Law Review.

19. For more guidance on ellipses, *see id.* and Garner, *The Redbook: A Manual on Legal Style* 27–30.

Appendix

Reader's Exercise Key

These are not *the* answers to the exercises. They are some of the many possible answers. Your answer may often be better than the one given here. That should be cause for cheer, not puzzlement.

❧ Exercise 1

Remember that the distinction between working words and glue words is rough-hewn, and reasonable people can differ about particular words in a sentence. Thus, don't worry if your answers aren't exactly like the ones suggested here.

1. Here is the original sentence with the working words underlined:

There are <u>three</u> <u>reasons</u> <u>given</u> in the <u>majority</u> <u>opinion</u> for its <u>rejection</u> of the <u>approach</u> <u>taken</u> by the <u>Supreme</u> <u>Court</u> in its <u>earlier</u> <u>decisions</u> with <u>respect</u> to the <u>Confrontation</u> <u>Clause</u> of the <u>Sixth</u> <u>Amendment.</u> (34 words total/ 17 working words)

The original sentence could be revised to read:

The <u>majority</u> <u>opinion</u> <u>gives</u> <u>three</u> <u>reasons</u> for <u>rejecting</u> the <u>Supreme</u> <u>Court's</u> <u>approach</u> in <u>earlier</u> <u>decisions</u> <u>concerning</u> the <u>Sixth</u> <u>Amendment's</u> <u>Confrontation</u> <u>Clause.</u> (21 words total/ 16 working words)

2. Here is the original sentence with the working words underlined:

A <u>motion</u> has been <u>made</u> by <u>Erickson</u> <u>seeking</u> <u>severance</u> of <u>his</u> <u>case</u> from the <u>action</u> against <u>Orrick</u> and the <u>proceedings</u> against <u>Sims</u>, and for a <u>trial</u> of <u>his</u> <u>case</u> <u>separate</u> from the <u>trial</u> of the <u>other</u> <u>two</u> <u>cases.</u> (38 words total/19 working words)

The original sentence could be revised to read:

<u>Erickson</u> has <u>moved</u> to <u>sever</u> <u>his</u> <u>case</u> and <u>try</u> it <u>separately</u> from the <u>Oxley</u> and <u>Sims</u> <u>cases.</u> (17 words total/ 10 working words)

3. Here is the original sentence with the working words underlined:

When <u>entering</u> into an <u>agreement</u> <u>regarding</u> the <u>settlement</u> of a <u>claim</u> <u>made</u> by a <u>client</u>, a <u>lawyer</u> <u>must</u> <u>not</u> <u>offer</u> or <u>agree</u> to a <u>provision</u> that <u>imposes</u> a <u>restriction</u> of the <u>right</u> of the <u>lawyer</u> to <u>practice</u> <u>law</u>, <u>including</u> the <u>right</u> to <u>undertake</u> <u>representation</u> of or <u>take</u> <u>particular</u> <u>actions</u> on <u>behalf</u> of <u>other</u> <u>clients</u> or <u>potential</u> <u>clients</u> with <u>similar</u> or <u>different</u> <u>claims</u> (62 words total/34 working words)

The original sentence could be revised to read:

In <u>settling</u> a <u>client's</u> <u>claim</u>, a <u>lawyer</u> <u>must</u> <u>not</u> <u>offer</u> or <u>make</u> an <u>agreement</u> that <u>restricts</u> the <u>lawyer's</u> <u>right</u> to <u>practice</u> <u>law</u>, <u>including</u> the <u>right</u> to <u>represent</u> or <u>act</u> for <u>other</u> <u>persons</u>. (32 words total/ 20 working words)

4. Here is the original sentence with the working words underlined:

The <u>conclusion</u> that was <u>reached</u> in <u>1954</u> by the <u>United</u> <u>States</u> <u>Supreme</u> <u>Court</u> in the <u>case</u> of <u>Brown</u> v. <u>Board</u> of <u>Education</u> of <u>Topeka</u> was that the <u>maintenance</u> of a "<u>separate</u> <u>but</u> <u>equal</u>"

education system in which segregation of children in the public schools solely on the basis of race is practiced, not withstanding the fact that the physical facilities and other tangible factors of the separate schools might be, or were in fact, equal, brings about a deprivation of the children from the minority group of equal opportunities with respect to education and thus causes a denial of equal protection of the laws, which is guaranteed to those children by the Fourteenth Amendment. (114 words total/ 59 working words)

The original sentence could be revised to read:

In *Brown v. Board of Education of Topeka* (1954), the United States Supreme Court concluded that a "separate but equal" education system is inherently unequal. Such a system segregates public school children solely by race. Even if the physical facilities and other tangible features of the minority children's schools are in fact equal, the segregation itself deprives the minority children of equal educational opportunities, thus denying them equal protection of the laws, in violation of the Fourteenth Amendment. (78 words total/ 52 working words)

∾ Exercise 2

1. To control how his art collection could be displayed after his death, the doctor created a very restrictive trust, hoping to keep everything exactly as it was during his lifetime.

2. Concerning the taxpayer's enormous charitable gift deduction, she did not submit an appraisal of the donated bronze sculpture. Therefore, we propose to disallow the deduction, as the Revenue Department's standard operating procedure requires.

3. The plaintiff seeks relief similar to a mandatory injunction. Before the merger of law and equity, that kind of relief could be granted only by Chancery.

4. At present, we have no legal remedy because the statute of limitations has run.

5. Based on the affidavits the parties filed with their cross-motions for summary judgment, we conclude that there are contested issues of fact; accordingly, we cannot issue summary judgment now.

6. For judicial economy's sake, we submit that this court should consolidate all nine civil actions, both for discovery now and for trial later.

∾ Exercise 3

1. Under the copyright license …

2. When the escrow closes …

3. Mandatory injunctive relief is inappropriate here …

4. After her release from prison, she was confined at home for at least six months.

5. Doubtless His Honor must recuse himself.

6. The action was barred because the statute of limitations period had expired.

7. The Court of Appeal must consider whether …

8. Until the design review committee approves the plans, the rules of the homeowner association prohibit you from starting construction.

9. Usually the insurance adjuster will start by denying the claim.

10. An attorney can be disciplined for suing without a good faith belief that the claim is legally and factually sound, and both the attorney and the client are subject to litigation sanction as well.

❧ Exercise 4

1. A person might make a significant gift to charity for three related reasons.

2. First, the person might simply want to aid the charity in question.

3. Second, the person might want to avoid capital gains tax by giving the charity an asset that is now much more valuable than it was when the person acquired it.

4. Third, if the person is very wealthy, a large charitable gift can reduce the estate tax that must be paid when the person dies.

5. Tax lawyers and estate planners should show their clients how their natural desire to give to charity can also reduce their taxes.

❧ Exercise 5

An agent owes a duty to the principal to act with the care, competence, and diligence that are normally exercised by agents of ordinary skill and prudence in similar circumstances. An agent's special skills or special knowledge are facts to consider in deciding whether the agent acted properly. Moreover, an agent has a duty to act only within the scope of the agent's actual authority. An agent must comply with all lawful instructions from the principal (or persons previously designated by the principal) concerning the agent's actions on the principal's behalf.

○ Exercise 6

1. An insurance claims agent should not lightly reject a policy holder's facially valid claim.

2. Rather, the claims agent should carefully consider the possible consequences.

3. Every contract – including an insurance contract – contains an implied term that the parties will deal fairly and act in good faith.

4. When a claims agent bluntly refuses to explain reasonably why the company will not pay a facially valid claim, that makes us question the agent's good faith.

5. The duty of good faith requires an insurance company to respond coherently to a facially valid claim.

6. The claims agent continued his "stonewall" tactic for 10 months, from which we infer that the agent intended to stall until the policy holder either capitulated or hired a lawyer.

○ Exercise 7

1. The new state statute <u>required</u> [active] Blanchard to register as a sex offender because, thirty-five years earlier, he <u>had been convicted</u> [passive] of forcing a minor to orally copulate him, a felony.

2. Twelve years after Blanchard <u>was released</u> [passive] from prison for that first offense, he <u>brandished</u> [active] a stick at an armored police vehicle during an anti-abortion demonstration, for which he <u>was convicted</u> [passive] of a felony— threatening serious bodily harm to a police officer. He <u>served</u>

[active]18 months in state prison for that offense, and he <u>was released</u> [passive] in 1987.

3. On June 30th of last year, the new sex offender registration statute <u>went</u> [active] into effect. It <u>required</u> [active] Blanchard to register within 30 days, and Blanchard <u>did</u> [active] so on July 15th.

4. The registration statute <u>requires</u> [active] every registered person to "update" the registration within five days following his or her birthday. Blanchard's birthday <u>is</u> [active] July 17th. Nothing significant <u>happened</u> [active] in Blanchard's life between July 15th and July 30th. Neither his address, nor his telephone number, nor his employment, nor any of his other registration data <u>changed</u> [active] between those two dates.

5. On July 30th, Blanchard <u>was arrested</u> [passive] by Police Lieutenant Lacy (one of the officers who <u>was sitting</u> [active] in the armored police vehicle when Blanchard <u>brandished</u> [active] the stick many years earlier). Blanchard <u>was arrested</u> [passive] for failing to "update" his sex offender registration between July 17th and July 22nd, as the registration statute <u>requires</u> [active]. The registration statute <u>makes</u> [active] failure to update an independent felony.

6. At his trial before a judge, Blanchard's counsel <u>argued</u> [active] that Blanchard <u>did not need</u> [active] to "update" his registration, because nothing <u>had changed</u> [active] in the few days since his registration on July 15th. The trial judge <u>rejected</u> [active] that argument and <u>found</u> [active] Blanchard guilty.

7. Our state's so-called "Three Strikes" law <u>permits</u> [active] a person to be sentenced from 25 years to life for a third felony, and the trial judge <u>sentenced</u> [active] Blanchard to 40 years in state prison. On this appeal, we <u>must decide</u> [active] whether that sentence <u>is</u> [active] so disproportionate to the gravity of Blanchard's offense as to constitute cruel or un-

usual punishment in violation of the Eighth Amendment or its counterpart in our state constitution.

ॐ Exercise 8

1. The stock exchange suspended trading in the defendant corporation's stock at 10:17 the following morning.

2. Neither the depositor nor anyone else notified the bank that the ATM card had been stolen. (The truncated passive voice at the end of the sentence is proper because we don't know who stole the ATM card.)

3. A farmer must fill in Dept. of Agriculture Form 9-2018 and bring it to any USDA branch office before planting any genetically modified sugar-beet seed in an open field.

4. After 180 days, either party can terminate this Agreement.

5. The Border Patrol Officer discovered two kilograms of an unidentified white powder in the spare tire well of Defendant's Volvo sedan.

6. You can deduct charitable gifts of appreciated assets at their fair market value at the time of the gift, and in that way you can avoid capital gains tax.

ॐ Exercise 9

1. In a tort case, an actor is not liable for harm that is different from the harms whose risks made the actor's conduct tortious. Likewise, an actor is not liable for harm when the tortious aspect of the actor's conduct did not increase the risk of harm. But sometimes an actor's tortious conduct causes harm to a person that, because of the person's physical or mental condition or other characteristic, is of a greater mag-

nitude or different type than might reasonably be expected. In that event, the actor is liable for all such harm to the person. (97 words, average sentence length 24 words)

2. The law of sentencing criminal offenders should have three goals. First, sentencing should be severe enough to reflect the gravity of the offense and the blameworthiness of the offender. Second, where success is reasonably likely, sentencing should seek to rehabilitate the offender, deter future offenses, incapacitate dangerous offenders, and restore crime victims and communities. Third, sentencing should be no more severe than is necessary to achieve the first two goals. (70 words, average sentence length 18 words)

3. The law of "gifts to a class of people" treats in vitro fertilization in the following way. If a husband and wife use in vitro fertilization to produce a child, the sperm sometimes comes from the husband and sometimes from a third party. Likewise, the eggs sometimes come from the wife and sometimes from a third party. A child produced from the husband's sperm and the wife's eggs is the genetic child of the husband and wife and is treated as their child for class-gift purposes. Suppose that a child is produced from a third party's sperm or a third party's eggs, with the embryo being placed in the wife's uterus. The child is the genetic child of the sperm or egg donor, but for class-gift purposes it is treated as the child of the husband and wife, not the third-party sperm or egg donor. (145 words, average sentence length 24 words)

ᐒ Exercise 10

1. Sometimes a property owner asks the building contractor to deviate substantially from the plans and specifications pre-

viously agreed upon. The building contractor may charge a reasonable amount extra for the deviation.

2. What if a lawyer offers her client's testimony, believing it to be true, but later learns that it is false? In that case, the lawyer must take "reasonable remedial measures."

3. The first of these "reasonable remedial measures" is for the lawyer to speak with the client in confidence. The lawyer should tell the client about the lawyer's duty of truthfulness to the court and should try to get the client to correct or withdraw the false testimony. *See Restatement (Third) of the Law Governing Lawyers* §120 (2000); American Bar Association Model Rules of Professional Conduct, Rule 3.3.

4. The lawyer should always try to cause the least harm to the client and the client's lawful objectives. If the first remedial step, described above, doesn't work, then the lawyer should consider withdrawing as counsel, if that will undo the effects of the client's false testimony.

5. If, and only if, the first two remedial steps fail, the lawyer must disclose the falsehood to the tribunal. That is a drastic step because it allows the lawyer, when necessary, to disclose information that would otherwise be privileged or protected by the ethical duty of confidentiality, or both.

∾ Exercise 11

A home owners' association that is chartered by South Carolina must act within the limits set by the following:
- its own charter; and
- the Constitution and laws of South Carolina; and
- the Constitution and laws of the United States.

Within those limits, such an association has the implied power to make reasonable rules for either or both of the following purposes:

- to govern use of the members' common property;
- to govern members' use of their individual property to protect the common property.

In addition to the implied power described above, such an association's charter may give it express power to make reasonable rules to protect members' individual property from unreasonable interference that is caused by either or both of the following:

- other members' use of the common property;
- other members' use of their individually owned property.

ᔆ Exercise 12

1. The airline's mechanics said that only the fuel tank had been repaired.

2. Counsel argued that the defendant, being fearful for her life, acted in self-defense.

3. Appellant's brief fails to consider the year 2005 changes to the pension provisions.

4. The trial judge held that the contract was void for lack of consideration.

5. The Department of Agriculture intended the new dairy regulations to reduce the open-air discharge of methane gas.

ᔆ Exercise 13

1. Conflicts of interest can seriously erode, if not entirely destroy, the relationship of trust between attorney and client. One attorney's conflict is usually imputed to all the other attorneys in the law firm.

2. One type of conflict of interest is where an attorney enters into any kind of business transaction with a client. That is a

conflict, even if the transaction is profitable for everyone. But the attorney can solve the conflict by making sure that four conditions are met.

3. First, the terms of the transaction must be fair and reasonable to the client, and the attorney must disclose the terms to the client, in writing, using clear, plain language.

ॐ Exercise 14

1. An attorney is allowed to reveal a client's confidential information to prevent serious financial injury due to a crime the client is about to commit, or to prevent death or serious bodily injury.

2. You can impeach a witness with a prior criminal conviction if it was a misdemeanor that involved dishonesty or false statement, or if it was a felony.

3. A corporation is liable for an investor's financial losses due to the criminal conduct of an officer or employee if that person was both (a) high-ranking, and (b) acting within the scope of his or her authority.

ॐ Exercise 15

1. In *Simpson v. Union Oil Co.*, Justice William O. Douglas said, but did not prove, that: "The patent laws which give a seventeen-year monopoly on 'making, using, or selling the invention' concern the same general subject as the antitrust laws, and the two should be construed together. The patent laws modify the antitrust laws to some extent. That is why *General Electric* was decided as it was."

2. To make the small-loan market more efficient in Central America, we need to find better ways for lenders to share in-

formation on defaults by borrowers, without encouraging lenders to restrain trade by agreeing among themselves on interest rates and risk assessment.

3. Cecil Wickham, Q.C.,* entered his appearance for the plaintiff, and defendant Augustine Crump entered his appearance on his own behalf.

◌ Exercise 16

1. The Company must indemnify and hold harmless each person who is or was a member of the Compensation Committee or Board of Directors from any loss, expense, or liability that is imposed upon, or reasonably incurred by, that person in connection with any proceedings (of whatever kind) in which that person is a party or is otherwise involved because of any act or failure to act under this Plan.

2. For an Employee, "Termination of Service" means any ending of the employer-employee relationship with the Company for any reason, including but not limited to, resignation, discharge, death, disability, or retirement.

3. Here is the original passage written by Warren Buffett, the plain-spoken head of Berkshire Hathaway, Inc., in its 2004 Annual Report:

Over the past 35 years, American business has delivered terrific results. It should therefore have been easy for investors to earn juicy returns: All they had to do was piggyback Cor-

---

* In British Commonwealth nations, Q.C. is a commonly recognized abbreviation for Queen's Counsel, the highest rank of barrister. The Queen appoints Queen's Counsel on advice of the Lord Chancellor. Only about 10% of barristers become Queen's Counsel. When the monarch is a King, the abbreviation is K.C.

porate America in a diversified, low-expense way. An index fund that they never touched would have done the job. Instead many investors have had experiences ranging from mediocre to disastrous.

❧ Exercise 17

1. As a trial lawyer, you are subject to local court rules. These concern efficient court administration, such as what size paper to use for court documents. You are also subject to the preferences of individual judges, such as whether you are to sit or stand when questioning a witness. But most important, you are subject to the rules of legal ethics that apply in court proceedings. For example, you must not take a frivolous legal position – one that you cannot support under the current law or by a good faith argument for changing the law. Likewise, you must not state your personal opinion about the justness of a cause, or the culpability of a litigant, or the credibility of a witness, and you must not make legal arguments that are not supported by evidence in the record.

2. a. strategies for managing insurance claims
   b. directives concerning corporate governance after the Sarbanes-Oxley Act
   c. proposals for research programs to prevent terrorism
   d. protocols for treating injuries from intramural sports
   e. regimen for symptomatic relief of prenatal stress

3. This homeowner's insurance policy does not cover losses caused by the following perils, even if some other cause contributed to the loss:
   ✓ freezing of interior pipes when the exterior temperature is at or above 32 degrees F.;
   ✓ a continuous or repeated leak of water or steam from some source other than the following items while they are

still under manufacturer's warranty: (a) a furnace, (b) an air conditioner, or (c) a fire sprinkler system;

✓ a mechanical breakdown that is caused by the insured's negligence

4. If we land in the water (which isn't likely), you will find an inflatable life jacket under your seat. When the flight attendant gives you the signal, take out your life jacket and put it on with the opening at the front, like an ordinary jacket. Buckle the nylon straps snugly around your waist. *Do not* inflate your life jacket until the flight attendant tells you to. After the flight attendant gives you the signal, use both hands to pull down gently on the two red tabs on the front. That will inflate the life jacket. Continue to do what the flight attendant tells you.

5. The defendant corporation set out to lie to people who own little and who have little scientific knowledge. To earn more profits for itself, the defendant used false advertising, hoping to convince these people that antiretroviral drugs cause impotence, and that defendant's vitamin pills are better than antiretrovirals in combating HIV.

6. a. Judges may examine witnesses who were called by the parties, and they may also call witnesses whom the parties have not called.

   b. A prosecutor may sometimes inveigle the judge to call a hostile but essential witness whom the prosecutor needs but fears to call. Questioning such a witness from the bench often salves the witness's hostility and makes him or her a more useful witness.

   c. Art. II, § 2, makes the President the Commander-in-Chief of the Army and Navy. It also empowers the President to grant reprieves and pardons for offenses against the United States. Therefore, if you were President, you could apparently order an Army or Navy officer to covertly violate a federal criminal statute and then, if the officer is caught and prosecuted, you could issue a pardon.

℃ Exercise 18

1. From 1776 until the end of the War of 1812, the overriding question was whether the nation – besieged without by hostile governments and within by provincialism – had sufficient power to survive.

2. During those formative years, the weakest of the three branches of government was the judiciary.

3. Not particularly brightening the outlook, President Adams's appointment of John Marshall to the Court in 1801 was unenthusiastically supported, even by the Federalists.

4. Yet, in its first 10 years under John Marshall's guidance, the Court consolidated far-reaching judicial power, and in another 15 it put Congress's authority on a broad and permanent constitutional footing.

5. The Jeffersonians were certain of two things: that the Constitution was a limiting document, and that John Marshall was a malignant force.

6. They charged the Chief Justice with usurping power and with converting his weak-willed colleagues to his plans for aggrandizement.

7. The Federalists, on the other hand, expected the Court to consolidate national power and contain the emerging forces of democracy.

8. There is precedent for non-judicial action by allies against a former enemy leader whose acts seem abhorrent: that of Napoleon.

9. When Napoleon escaped from Elba, broke the 1814 peace treaty, and marched again on Europe, he was declared "*hors la loi*," that is, "beyond the law," by representatives of all the European states, except France. That left the question what to do about him.

10. The Prussians said "shoot him," and the Russians said, more delicately, "summary execution."

11. Ultimately, however, the Europeans agreed to exile him to St. Helena, where he would be out of the way and kept at British expense.

12. Exile spared the embarrassment of executing a sovereign. All European rulers had condemned the execution of Louis XVI and did not want their subjects to suppose that killing rulers was an acceptable way of expressing their opinion of them.

13. No one seriously considered a trial for Napoleon; it was unnecessary since his crimes were self-evident, condemnation was universal, and the European leaders had no qualms about punishing him for them.

14. However, the idea of a trial for Nazi war criminals was attractive to many, even though the form the proponents favored was repugnant to others.

15. Stalin had punished his opponents and frightened others by "show trials" in the 1930s, and Hitler himself mounted a show trial for those who plotted to take his life in July 1944.

16. In a show trial, one can even allow a little defense – just enough to demonstrate how feeble it is.

17. The U.S. Supreme Court has held that the processing and disposal of solid waste in landfills concerns an article of commerce for purposes of Commerce Clause analysis.

18. The legal issue in this case is whether the article-of-commerce test is satisfied when applied to sewage sludge, the substance in question here.

19. Sewage sludge is a by-product of wastewater treatment. It is generally a solid or semi-solid, mud-like substance, typically consisting of water and from 2% to 28% solids.

20. Some people limit the term "sewage sludge" to mean stabilized, disinfected sewage sludge that is suitable for beneficial agricultural uses.

21. Sewage sludge differs from solid waste, in that economic, ecological, and agricultural benefits are realized by farmers using treated sewage sludge as fertilizer.

22. If solid waste constitutes an article of commerce, an even stronger, more persuasive case can be made for regarding sewage sludge as an article of commerce for Commerce Clause purposes.

23. Plaintiff Lutz sued defendant Reliance Nissan for wrongful termination, and defendant successfully moved to compel arbitration pursuant to a two-tiered arbitration procedure that was specified by her employment contract.

24. Lutz won the initial arbitration, but upon a second-tier review, the "appellate" arbitrator reversed Lutz's award and entered an award for defendant, which award was confirmed by the trial court.

25. In a premature appeal from the trial court's confirmation order, Lutz raises various meritless arguments.

26. We hold that Lutz is responsible for the delay of which she complains; that she suffered no harm, because defendant paid for all arbitration costs; that the two-tiered procedure (which is uncommon but not unconscionable) was contractually

binding; and, most important, that the contract permissibly invested the "appellate" arbitrator with a broader standard of review than an appellate court would ordinarily have.

27. Our economic system depends, in part, on legal recognition of property rights and the ability of parties to enforce contract rights when necessary. (The commas are optional.)

28. (The original sentence is punctuated properly.)

29. (The original sentence is punctuated properly.)

30. Attorney conflicts of interest can arise with present clients, prospective clients, and former clients.

31. The most common causes of attorney discipline are alcohol and greed.

32. (The original sentence is punctuated properly.)

33. (The original sentence is punctuated properly.)

34. Our deadline is [or deadline's] shorter now, because of the one-year statute of limitations.

35. The people's right to be secure in their persons, houses, papers, and effects, against unreasonable searches and seizures shall not be violated.

36. It's important to listen to our instincts when assessing a legal argument's validity.

37. (The original sentence is punctuated properly.)

38. Justice O'Connor's concurring opinion took issue with the majority's reliance on cases from the 1920s, before the expansion of Congress's power under the Commerce Clause. Hers is the more persuasive of the two opinions.

39. A business's net worth is not always a good measure of its future profitability.

40. Microsoft's Bill Gates's public image improved when his contributions to various charitable and educational causes increased.

41. "Whose brown satchel is that beside the witness stand, and what is [or what's] it doing there?" asked the judge in a quiet voice.

Index and Lawyer's Word Guide